Better Golf Tips

Golf tips, tricks and drills.

Over 200 pages of stroke saving tips and game improvement drills. A comprehensive guide, especially written for the recreational player and guaranteed to make any sick golf game better.

"Doctor" Nick

For absent friends, Albert,
Edward and Ray.

CONTENTS

Introduction 9

About this book 15

The four games of golf 16

The new ball flight laws 18

THE LONG GAME 23

The secret of good golf 25

Swing tips and tricks 53

Swing drills 91

THE SHORT GAME 131

Putting 133

Chipping 151

Bunkers 169

Pitching   175

Scoring tips   181

MANAGING YOUR MIND   185

Tips to improve your mental game

MANAGING YOUR GAME   209

Ideas to help you find your best score each day

JUNIOR GOLF   233

The next generation

ACKNOWLEDGEMENTS   238

Introduction

About "Doctor" Nick

Now – I am not a medical doctor (and I have never been in the "Simpson's" cartoon series) but many of my friends, colleagues and clients call me "Doctor" Nick, because, if your golf game is unwell or your putting is poorly, if you choke on your chip shots or you are just sick of playing bad golf – "Doctor" Nick can make you better.

Okay, I admit it's a bit much and that my unpronounceable surname may have encouraged the use of an easy alternative. However, most clients feel (I am told) that the nickname is appropriate because I really do cure sick golf games. My name is Nick Obolewicz (pronounced Obo – lev – itch); I am English although I was brought up in St Andrews, Scotland, where I first learned to play golf. From an early age I wanted to be a golf professional, but not a Tour player or a Club pro in a shop. The moment I realised that even the best players in the world have someone who guides their game, I knew I wanted to teach our great game. Since then I have been wonderfully lucky in learning my craft.

First, at my Dad's insistence (so I would have a back-up plan), I qualified and was successful as a training consultant, which gave me a wealth of essential information about presentation, communication, training, coaching and evaluation. These are skills that I employ daily with my clients as well as when I am developing and delivering courses for the next generation of golf teaching professionals. Second, because I learned to play at a time when there was little formal instruction available, I very much figured out the golf swing on my own. As a result and unlike many modern pros who have started with and maintained perfect golf swings, it seems I have had (and cured) every swing error there is.

From this I have not only learned how to fix the problem, but also how it is caused and what it feels like. That experience is valuable and pretty unique. For my clients, it is like going to your G.P. with a mystery illness and discovering that he or she has had, diagnosed and cured the same ailment. Third, I have a logical and analytical mind with a voracious appetite for new information. Nobody can learn to be a great golf teacher on their own and I am proud to say that I stand on the shoulders of giants. I have studied and worked with many great coaches, attended hundreds of courses and presentations and read thousands of books from those professionals and teachers who are unreachable by geography or who have passed away. Fourth, by swinging the club poorly (by my standards) for many years, I learned how to score through good course management, mind management and a magical short game developed through necessity and hours spent "messing about" with a rusty wedge. Finally, I have been teaching golf for over 30 years – mostly at golf clubs and driving ranges, so the vast majority of my daily clients are recreational players. Big name coaches who work with top players (golf's athletes) publish most of the books on the golf swing. Those books are great if you are also an athlete with a personal trainer and unlimited access to the golf range. Most of my clients sit at a desk all day, do regular jobs, are busy mums or drive for a living and golf is sometimes their only exercise, so my coaching has to work for them (and it does).

"Doctor" Nick – Golf Professional, Woodstock Golf Club, Ennis, Co. Clare, Ireland

"Doctor" Nick's

Golf tips, tricks and drills.

About this book

This book is perhaps a little different to the usual golf books. It is not the latest swing secret, putting bible or master class in sports psychology. It is a collection of tips, tricks and drills that I have written and had published over the last few years. Although many golfers would benefit from a swing rebuild and structured programme of development, the truth is that most do not have the time, commitment or money to put into a process that can take even top players two to three years to complete. In practice, most recreational players try different tips and ideas they pick up from magazines or golf shows. Many of my clients have read my instructional series "To the Fore" and asked if I would ever put the tips into one book, so I did. This book contains some of the most popular tips from the series, with each page being a separate tip, drill or collection of connected thoughts. You can read this book from cover to cover or just flick through. The choice is yours.

If you came to me for a golf lesson, then I could easily recommend the correct drill or tip for you, a bit like your doctor prescribing some medication. Think of this book as being your own little golf medicine cabinet where you can choose which pills to try, or not. Although the wrong pill will not help you at all and some may not help very much, most will make your golf a lot better and, who knows, you may just have fun along the way.

To help you find the correct medicine for what ails your game, I have grouped the tips together into what I consider to be, the four "games" that are golf. I hope you find my book useful and have as much fun reading it, as I did in putting it together.

Happy golfing!

The four games of golf.

Many golfers make the mistake, of thinking that golf is all about hitting full shots, (and a bit of putting). They believe that, if they improve their swing, they will magically play better golf. Successful golfers know, that there are four "games" in golf, and you need to work at all of them, to improve. Very often, I find that improving the correct area of the game can yield significant improvements, almost immediately. Look at the four "games" below, and ask yourself if 25% of your golfing time is applied to each area? The tips, tricks, and drills, in this book, are grouped into these four headings, to help you find your "cure" quickly.

1: The long game.

Every shot you hit and swing you make from outside 100 yards from the green. If you practice golf for an hour a week, then you should only spend 15 minutes on your full swing.

2: The short game.

Every shot you hit from inside 100 yards from the green. This includes putting, chipping, pitching and bunker play. If you practice golf for four hours a week, then you should spend one hour on your short game, it's the scoring zone.

3: Mind management.

A golfer with a good mind and a poor swing will usually beat the golfer with a good swing who thinks poorly. Learning how to control their emotions and thinking better, will save most golfers half their handicap in shots.

4: Game management.

Preparation, practice, time management, diet, fitness, hydration, flexibility and course management are some of the crucial areas to consider. Swapping two hours of golf for the correct type of practice could make your game 25% more enjoyable.

The New Ball Flight Laws

At one time, most people thought the earth was flat and we now know it isn't. The change doesn't matter to most people that much, unless you are a rocket scientist. However, imagine trying to drive a car, if you believed that the gear stick directed the car and the steering wheel changed the gears — messy! There is a fundamental misunderstanding of what happens when a golf club strikes the ball (known as "The Ball Flight Laws") and it is causing many golfers to try and change the wrong thing, when the ball does not go where they expect. I would like to introduce you to The New Ball Flight Law in the hope that this little change in understanding will have a profound effect on your golf.

For almost the entire history of golf instruction, and certainly since the publication of John Jacobs' Practical Golf in 1972, the ball flight laws have been set in stone. The PGA manual of golf, and generations of golf professionals have believed that, a well struck golf shot will start on the path that the club was swinging along, then change direction towards where the clubface was looking at impact. Many top teachers still believe that the swing path controls the initial direction of the ball flight. This assumption is fundamental to the teaching theory of all of the major teaching organisations, as well as being built into the software of most golf simulators. There is now clear evidence that this theory is outdated and needs to change. Recently some teachers have put forward the theory that the ball will leave the clubface in exactly the direction it is looking, then bend because of the sidespin applied by the club path. If golf ball development were to continue unchecked, this theory may eventually be correct. However, at present the correct ball flight law should be that:

A well-struck ball will always leave the clubface at close to the direction it was facing, then change direction relative to the differential between the clubface and club path at impact.

Or, if you prefer:

"The clubface sends it, and the differential bends it."

As a golfer, you really only need to know two things.

1. The direction that the ball went when you hit it, is where the clubface was pointed, and the swing path (by cutting across the aim of the clubface) causes any subsequent curve.
2. That your golf teacher understands the new ball flight laws.

For most golfers, you now know all you need to know, and you can go off and read something else. However, if you are keen to know the technical details – read on.

I want to be clear, the original theory was (probably) correct and this is supported by many years of successful teaching. It is outdated now because of the changes in modern equipment - in particular "hotter" golf balls and clubfaces. The modern golf ball flies much further and straighter than the 3-piece soft balata balls, common in the 1950's to the 80's. But technology has changed the game, and has also altered the ball flight laws. There is a lot of complicated physics effecting the collision between the club and ball, but the most important element is easiest to understand and that is the change in the elasticity of the ball.

If you drop a golf ball at arms length onto a hard surface, it will rebound, but to a slightly lower height; this is because some of the energy is absorbed through the elastic properties of the ball. The amount of the rebound is at a constant rate over a large range of speeds and is known as the coefficient of restitution, or COR. So a ball dropped from 10 feet that rebounds to 7 feet has a COR of 0.7 and will rebound to 14 feet if dropped from 20 feet. A perfectly inelastic ball (if one were ever to exist) would have a COR of one, and a ball of putty would have a COR of almost zero, not rebounding at all. You could describe the effect of a lower COR as allowing the ball to stay in contact with the colliding surface for longer; this rule also applies to angled collisions. It is a fact that the COR of golf balls has changed over the last 30 years. There is even a considerable variation between the balls available today. I recently tested two golf balls to try and illustrate this change in elasticity over the years. A modern ball dropped from 60 inches rebounded consistently to 44 inches, giving a COR of 0.73. Whereas a balata ball from 1990 dropped from the same height, only rebounded to 36 inches, giving a COR of 0.60 – a substantial difference!

It is easy then, to visualise a high-speed video of a clubface striking objects where the face is (for example) 10 degrees open to the path. If you were to hit a steel ball it would leave the clubface almost instantly at 10 degrees to the path, but strike a ball of putty and it will remain on the clubface and travel along the path, at zero degrees. We may also observe that the cushioning effect of the sand during a bunker shot, will reduce the COR of the golf ball, allowing it to follow the club path for longer. A ball from the 1950's may have had a COR of less than 0.5, and probably would have followed the club path for some time, before changing direction quite violently, because of the sidespin created during the impact. The modern ball, however, when struck solidly, will compress on the clubface then rebound at slightly less than the angle of the clubface, but it will not follow the path of the club. I have several high-speed videos that clearly show the ball leaving the clubface, at close to the angle of the face (9.23 degrees, when the face was 10 degrees open), the angle varies depending on the ball used and the type of club, but the average is around 85% of the clubface angle.

This change simplifies the teaching and analysis of ball flight considerably, because there is now only one club path (the actual club path relative to the clubface) and we no longer need to refer to the club path as being in to out, or out to in, of the imaginary target line. The clubface aim is now our primary concern, and the swing path is either square to the face or not, with the differential creating the sidespin and therefore movement, left or right. One of the most important changes this brings about, is that the ball will never cross the club path (unless it is moved by the wind). For a right-handed player, a ball struck with the face closed to the swing path, will always move to the left of the swing path immediately, and visa-versa. A ball struck with the face closed to the swing path, can never start to the right of the path (or even on it) and then move left, it can only moved left immediately.

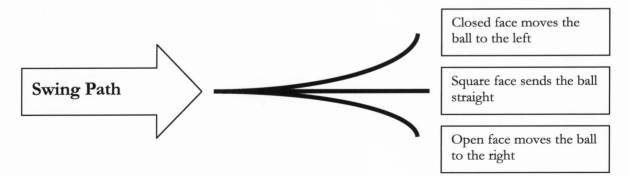

Swing Path

Closed face moves the ball to the left

Square face sends the ball straight

Open face moves the ball to the right

If we were to reintroduce the imaginary target line, then to hit a ball that starts to the right of the target line and draws back to the target, you would need the clubface to be open to the target line, but closed to the swing path.

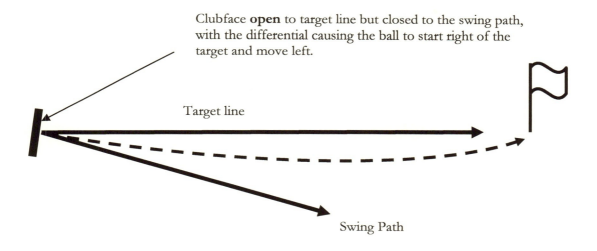

Clubface **open** to target line but closed to the swing path, with the differential causing the ball to start right of the target and move left.

Target line

Swing Path

To summarise, it is now clear that the golf balls we used many years ago, had a low COR and when combined with the equipment available, would probably create impact conditions that allowed the ball to follow the swing path, then move in the direction of the clubface. This created the current (flawed) ball flight laws. With the advent of modern balls and clubs that have high COR properties, the ball now immediately travels close to the direction the clubface was looking, then changes direction only if there is a differential between the clubface and the club path. Understanding this fact as a golfer will help you improve your game. Misunderstanding the ball flight law, as a golf teacher, would be like a rocket scientist still thinking the earth was flat. Make sure both you, and your golf coach, know the law!

The Long Game

At last – the secret of good golf!

As a junior golfer, I read hundreds of golf books, in the search of the elusive "secret of good golf". I even read some that claimed to hold the secret, and some that were called "The Secret of Golf". The first five chapters of most of those golf books were on the grip, aim, alignment, ball position and posture. Once I had read my first couple of books, I would skip forwards in search of the elusive "secret". Eventually I came to understand, that it was those five chapters, and finding the correct power source, that is the *real* secret of the consistent, repeatable swing.

The fundamentals of having a sound grip, aim, alignment, ball position, and posture, are crucial to building a good golf swing, in the same way that good foundations are needed to build a good house. Most of us have heard of the "Leaning Tower of Pisa", and you probably know that it leans because it has poor foundations. You may not know that the tower has a double lean. Because the foundations were so poor, it started to lean while they were building it, and in an effort to correct the problem, the builders added a kink. Of course, had they corrected the foundations at an early stage, the tower would not be subsiding, and still requiring repairs. Many golf swings are the same, with poor fundamentals being the bad foundations, leaving a swing that is constantly in need of repair and maintenance. It is a major undertaking to dismantle an established golf swing, so it can be rebuilt on sound foundations; it is clearly far better to start with good fundamentals. Please don't skip the fundamentals, make an effort to read each section twice – then go back and read them again. You will be glad you did.

Focus on what you <u>can</u> control.

I find that most amateur golfers are obsessed with trying to hit good golf shots, and they get very angry when they hit bad shots. However, they tend to be rather lax about the fundamentals of their set-up, assuming that they will "sort it out", during the swing. Conversely, professional golfers are constantly checking that their set-up is correct, but they are relatively relaxed about where the ball goes. This is because professional golfers understand that, 95% of poor shots begin with a mistake in the set-up, and that even the very best golfers, still make the occasional swing errors. By setting up correctly, you at least give yourself the best opportunity, to hit a good shot. You have total control over how you set up, so copy the pros, and get it right.

Over the next few pages I will be giving you some tips on each element of a good set-up. Take the time to check that each element of your set-up is correct, and recheck them frequently. By focusing on the things that you can control, before you swing, you may find a significant improvement in your ball striking.

A good grip – it's in your hands.

In golf, more than any other stick and ball game, a good grip is vital. Your hands are the only things, which attach you to the golf club and (because of the dynamic forces created during the swing), a small grip error, can cause spectacularly bad golf shots. Contrary to popular belief, you cannot "get away" with an incorrect grip, and square the clubface by instinct. The time taken to swing the club, from behind your head to impact, is actually less than the time it takes for the electrical signal to travel from your hands, to your brain, and back again. Most golfers who play with a grip that is incorrect (for them) develop several compensations, in their stance and swing, to try and get the ball heading in the right direction. Adding two or three errors to an already wonky grip will cause inconsistent golf, and waste power and talent. When I am teaching, I look for three things in any grip – pressure, placement, and pairing. Look at the points below, and see if you need to correct your grip. However, be warned, more than any other element of the swing, grip changes are hard work. Keep at it though, the secret to better golf, is right there in your hands.

Pressure.

The correct grip pressure, will allow your wrists to create, and release the correct angles in the swing, developing leverage, and increasing clubhead speed. Unless you are playing the ball from six inches of thick rough, you should grip the club with just enough pressure, to squeeze a tube of toothpaste. Or on a scale of one to 10 (with 10 being the tightest), you should grip with a pressure of three to four at most. Many golfers feel the need to grip the club fiercely, because the club is held incorrectly, and is therefore unstable in their hands. Now, lets check how you grip.

Placement.

By placing the club correctly in your fingers, it becomes a precision instrument, and not just a bat. Your left hand acts as an anchor, and is placed on the side of the club, so that it sits on your "life line", across your index finger, and under the heel of your hand. Your right hand is applied to the side of the grip, so the club sits across the base of the knuckle joints, and into the fingers. The index finger is "triggered" slightly away from the others. If your grip is correct, you should now be able to make fast, 360 degree, "helicopter" swings, over your head, without your hands slipping.

Pairing.

A correct grip will naturally "square" the clubface at impact, without any need for correction. To achieve this, your palms must face each other, and pair up without twisting. If I were wearing a watch in the first picture, the face of the watch would be looking directly at the target, at set-up, and impact. My hands are correctly paired so they work together in balance; notice that there is a slight cupping in the back of my left wrist. From this position, all I need to do is close my hands on the club and I will have a perfectly paired grip. In the second picture, the hands would be working in opposition, fighting each other throughout the swing and causing inconsistent shots. If you want to score well with a grip like this, then you will need to be a very lucky golfer and an excellent putter!

Get to work on your grip; better golf is in your hands.

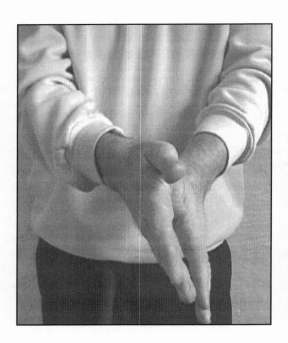 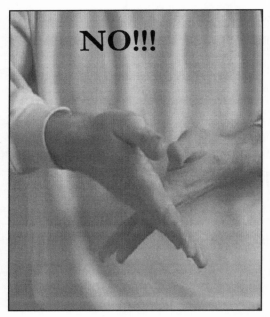

NO!!!

Get a grip - it's only natural.

A good grip does three things. First, it stops the club flying out of your hands (always embarrassing). Second, it permits your wrists to create correct leverage (maximising power) and third, it allows the club to return to the ball squarely without any correction by you. This is achieved by taking notice of how your hands and arms naturally "hang" and keeping the same angles once you grip the club. Be warned - more than any other element of the swing, grip changes are hard work. This is because you will be accustomed to what you currently do and it will feel most odd to make changes. However, stick to it and you will be surprised by how little you will need to consciously use your hands once you have a correct grip. Follow these easy steps to check and practice your grip. Reverse the instructions if you play left handed.

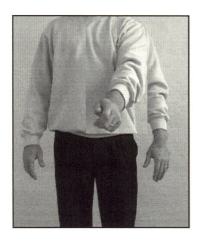 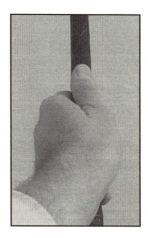

1. Looking in a mirror, let your arms hang loosely by your side then bring your left arm up keeping your hand at the same angle. Now hold a golf club in your left hand and match the angle. Usually you can do this by counting the number of knuckles you can see, in my case two and a half.

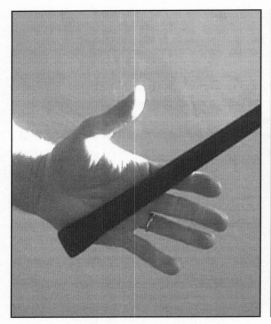 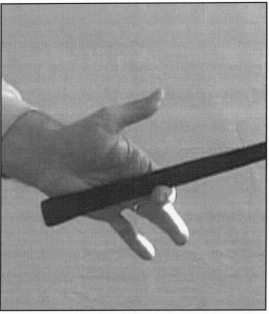

2. Your left hand is placed on the **side of the club** so that it sits on your "life line", across your index finger and under the heel of your hand. A good test of correct placement of your left hand is to try supporting the club with just the index finger. If the club slips off your hand it is not correctly placed.

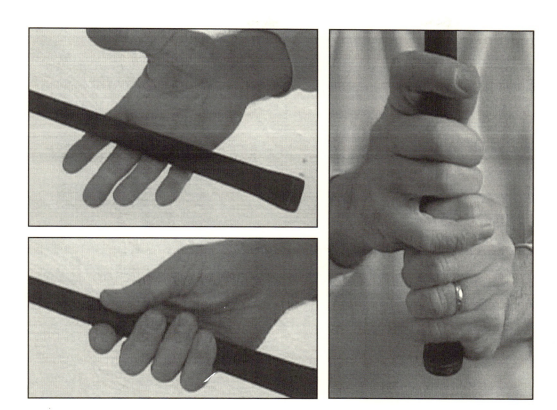

3. Your right hand is applied to the side of the grip so the club sits across the base of the knuckle joints and into the fingers. The index finger is "triggered" slightly away from the others. You can either overlap or interlock the little finger of the right hand; this is only done to reduce the strength of your right hand grip. Golfers who lack strength (ladies and children) should consider keeping all eight fingers on the club.

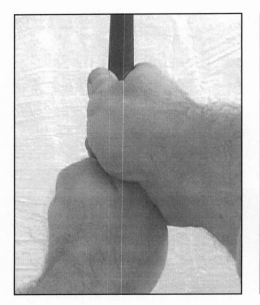
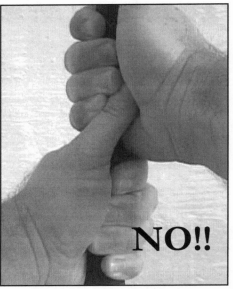

4. Once your grip is complete your left thumb should sit comfortably in the palm of your right hand and you should see two to three knuckles of your left hand and half to one on your right. If you see 2 handfuls of fingers then things are definitely wrong. Finally, you need to maintain a light consistent grip pressure throughout the swing, just below that required to break an egg will do just fine for most people.

Check your aim.

All golfers hit bad shots, and all golfers make bad swings. It's inevitable, because we are only human, and therefore fallible. All golfers also make good swings, and some make a lot of good swings. The sad thing is that the majority of recreational golfers, don't know when they make a good swing. This is because their aim is incorrect, and when they make a good swing they hit the ball exactly where they were aiming, and that was not where they wanted to go. Incorrect aim creates an unacceptable situation in golf, where the player needs to make a bad swing, to hit the ball on target. Correcting your aim is tremendously beneficial in golf. This is because, bad swings then result in poor shots, and good swings, are rewarded with good shots. This "positive feedback loop", is a natural aid to the evolution of a good swing. Now you are punished for incorrect actions, and rewarded for good, and naturally, you will find yourself doing more of the good swings.

Most golfers, including professionals, are unaware of when their aim gets off target. Typically, around 90% of the golfers I see for lessons and coaching, will need to correct their aim at some point. Once you know how to aim correctly, it is good practice, and simple, to check your own aim. The first thing to understand is that, the only thing that looks at the target in the set-up, is the bottom edge of the clubface. Everything else, that is, the lines through your feet, knees, hips, elbows, shoulders, and eyes, should align parallel left of the target (for a right-handed golfer).

Check your aim frequently by placing a club shaft along your toe-line, then look along the shaft to see if it points slightly left of your intended target.

Take dead aim.

In golf, your aim is simply where your clubface and body are pointing. Even the most accurate gun in the world will miss the target every time if it is pointed in the wrong direction. Your golf swing may not be the most accurate, but a good swing can only fire the ball at the target if you aim correctly. I see many golfers making the mistake of setting up to the ball first then looking for the target and trying to "twist" into some sort of aim. Professional golfers will start behind the ball, choosing an intermediate target (like a leaf or a discoloured tuft of grass) that is on the target line two to four feet away. They will then aim the clubface at the intermediate target and align their body with the correct target line. Correctly aimed, you should be able to turn your head and easily see the target, without looking over your shoulder.

1. Stand directly behind the ball and picture the shot you intend to hit. Select a small, precise target, not just "the fairway". Now pick an intermediate spot that is about three feet away and on your target line.

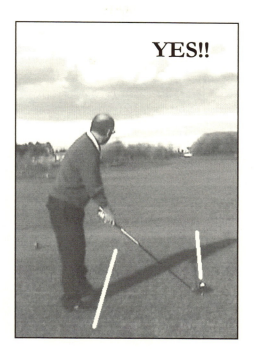

YES!!

2. Approach the ball with the club in your right hand (if you play right handed) and place your right foot forward. Now you can aim the clubface correctly at the target using the intermediate spot.

3. Once the clubface is aimed correctly, bring your body parallel to the target line and then grip the club. Check again that the club is aimed correctly using the intermediate and actual targets. **Perfect.**

Incorrect aim.

Here I am demonstrating a very common set-up error that creates bad aim, and inevitably leads to horrid golf shots. By approaching the ball with the club in my target side (left) hand, my left foot is pulled forward, closing my body to the intended target line. To see my target, I need to look over my shoulder, and that should always ring alarm bells, unless you are trying to hook the ball around a tree. If I make a good swing from this set-up, I will hit the ball 80 yards right of my intended target.

NO!!!

Train like a train – for good alignment.

Alignment in golf is simply how all the bits of your body align with each other, relative to the correct target line. It is important because your body will naturally try and return to correct alignment under the extreme stresses created during the golf swing. Even a small misalignment can have a major effect. Like a supermarket trolley with one "wobbly" wheel - fully laden it is almost impossible to keep in line. Many club golfers try to create good alignment, but incorrectly try and aim their body at the target. In golf, the only thing that points at the target is the clubface. Everything else, that is, the lines through your feet, knees, hips, shoulders, elbows and eyes, align parallel to the target line and therefore looking slightly left of the target (for a right-handed golfer). It may help to picture that you are a train with one wheel (the golf ball and club) on one railway line and the other wheel (your feet) are on the second line; the two lines are parallel but not pointing in exactly the same direction. Below is an example of good alignment and several common errors. Keep an eye on your alignment next time you play. You may be surprised how your game improves.

This is great alignment. My feet, knees, hips, shoulders, elbows and eyes are parallel left of the target line. I can make a good swing from this set-up.

(Actually I did. This shot hit the flag and dropped into the hole!)

The golf NCT – check your alignment now.

During the Irish National Car Test (NCT), your car's wheels are checked for alignment, to ensure all the tyres work together correctly. In the golf swing, alignment is how the lines through your feet, knees, hips, shoulders, elbows, eyes and clubface line up with each other – relative to your intended target. Good alignment is getting all the lines to run parallel to each other, when the clubface looks at the target. Better players, can deliberately change their alignment, to work the ball through the air, as in the example below. Here I am set up to turn the ball from left-to-right, around the dogleg. However, because the golf swing is very dynamic, and generates tremendous forces, your golf will quickly become inconsistent if you accidentally have poor alignment.

It's a bit like trying to drive a car on the motorway with a flat tyre – not easy.

Good alignment.

In the first three pictures below, I am hitting a driver at the wonderful seventh hole, at Woodstock golf club. In my set-up, all the alignment lines correctly point parallel left of my target (circled). In the second picture, at the top of my back swing, I am free to set the club correctly, parallel to my target line, and pointing directly at the target. All I need to do from here is uncoil my body, and release the club powerfully into the back of the ball. The third picture shows the "pre-impact position", with my feet, hips, knees, shoulders, and eyes, again parallel to my target. My elbows will line up at the moment of impact. Good alignment allows me to swing the club around my body, like a wheel in balance. If your golf is a little "wobbly", perhaps your alignment is off. Have your golf NCT, and get that alignment corrected. You will be delighted with the improvement.

Bad alignment.

In these pictures, I am demonstrating two common alignment errors. In the first picture, the ball is too far to my left, causing my shoulders and elbows to point to the left, of a good alignment position. Typically this golfer will hit a weak slice. In the second picture, the ball is too far right, causing my elbows and shoulders, to point to the right. If you must make a mistake, then this is preferable, as this golfer will tend to hit the ball with draw, from right to left. He will however, tend to hit the ball very low, and with an occasional, uncontrollable hook. It is easier to play with correct alignment. Give it a try.

Perfect your posture.

Good posture is essential, if you want any chance of making a decent golf swing. Your posture is simply the shape your body makes, when you are ready to swing the club. Great posture will put you in an athletic position, that allows you to turn around your spine, naturally creating speed and power, and returning the club squarely to the back of the ball. Players with good posture look balanced, and powerful, regardless of their age, or gender. I have two damaged discs low in my back, (unrelated to golf) and yet, as long as I maintain good posture I am able to play golf "full out" and without pain. Your posture may differ slightly, depending on your body shape, height, and swing type, but the basic checkpoints of a good posture are all the same.

Good Posture.

The three pictures below are from a real swing, in a competitive situation. I put this 7-iron to four feet.

Notice how my initial posture allows me to swing around my spine, without any changes in my height, relative to the background. In the first picture, there is a slight flex in my knees, and my weight is centred through my feet and well balanced. Also my arms are hanging freely, about one hand width away from my legs, and my chin is away from my chest. In the second and third pictures, notice how I am free to use my legs, below my body, to resist in the backswing, and to drive through impact. This initial posture helps me stay in "shape" throughout the swing; as a result, no power is wasted, by changes in height, or trying to keep in balance.

Check out your posture. It could be a quick fix to better golf.

Five steps to perfect posture.

Your posture is the "shape" you create when preparing to play a golf shot. Good posture is one of the five essential building blocks of a good swing. If you are able to stay in "shape" throughout your swing then the club will be returned precisely to the back of the ball without any need for correction or manipulation. This improved stability will make your swing more consistent and improve power - hitting the ball further, with less effort. More importantly, golfers with bad posture are likely to suffer with back, neck and knee problems to add to their bad golf shots. Creating good posture is easy. Follow these five simple steps and with a little practice you too will have perfect posture.

1. Stand erect with your back and legs straight. Hold a club in your right hand, with the toe pointing downwards.

2. Lift the club over your head and down your spine. Keep the club touching your head and your spine at the top and bottom.

3. Now hinge forward from your hip socket, keeping the club touching your head and spine. Keep your chin up.

4. Next, crack your knees to put a slight bend in your legs. Be careful not to create an excessive or substantial knee bend.

5. Finally, bring your arms and the club into position, allowing your arms to hang. Now "shuffle" forwards until the ball is in the way of the club.

That's perfect posture.

Two quick ways to a bad back.

Here are some typical examples of bad posture.

1. Here I have bent from the middle of my back, and pulled my hips forward. This is slouching. Even standing like this hurts my back.

2. In the second example, I am over-reaching for the ball, with my weight on my heels. It is impossible to maintain this position throughout the swing.

There is no easy way to hit good shots, from bad posture like this.

Ball position – more important than you may think.

Of the five essential elements of a good set-up, (the others being, grip, aim, posture and alignment), ball position, has the most potential for "cause and effect" changes, to ball flight.

Creating the correct ball position for your swing, takes a little effort, and a big chunk of common sense. However, if you take notice of the points below, you could soon be well on your way.

Cause and effect.

Almost 50 years ago, the great golf teacher, John Jacobs, frequently demonstrated his talent, during group lessons, where he corrected each person's shots, fixing hooks and slices, by only changing their ball position at set-up.

Amazingly, he would stand with his back to the golfer, and make the changes without looking at anything but the ball in flight.

It's a neat trick, but it does prove the importance of correct ball position.

Distance.

The first aspect of ball position to consider is, how far from the ball to stand. Obviously, the longer the club is, the further away you need to be. But, in general a good rule of thumb, is to ensure that the gap between the heel of your hand, and the top of your thighs, is around one hand's width, as in the picture below. From a decent posture, this would allow your arms to hang comfortably, below your shoulders.

If you stand too far from the ball, your posture will lean forwards, upsetting your balance, and creating an excessively flat swing. You will frequently top the ball, as you are unable to maintain your posture throughout the swing.

Conversely, a golfer who stands too close to the ball, will be inclined to swing too upright, and lack the room to swing the club freely through impact. In this case, you may hit the ground before the ball, or lack power and distance.

Both faults could cause the dreaded case of the "shanks" – where the ball is mishit with the neck of the golf club.

The next thing to consider is the ball position (left to right along the target line), relative to your feet.

Here the ball is too close, causing my posture to change. Swing from this position and your hips will get in your way, probably causing a shank.

This is a common error. The ball is too far away, causing the shaft to run up the line of my right forearm. It is very hard to make good swings from here.

Constant equals consistent.

Many club golfers use a different ball position on every shot. I encourage my clients to use a constant ball position on every normal shot. There are several reasons why I believe this is the best approach. Here are a few:

A constant ball position is easier to learn and repeat correctly.

In most golf sets, clubs are matched so they all swing the same. If you have a constant ball position, you will only need to learn one golf swing for all of your clubs. That must be easier.

Using a constant ball position will help you set up more consistently.

Many recreational golfers play their woods too far forward (to the left) and irons too far back (relative to the sternum). With the ball too far forward your shoulders will open at address, creating an out to in swing with an open face causing a weak slice. Playing with the ball too far to the right will result in blocked shots and hooks.

Some of golf's greatest players used a constant ball position, including Ben Hogan and Jack Nicklaus (and me!).

Let the length of your club decide how far you stand from the ball. If you position the ball just inside your left heel (for a right handed golfer), then you only need to move your right foot, to set the width of your stance. The gap between your heels should be about eight inches for a sand-wedge, becoming around half an inch wider (by moving your right foot), further for each club. Try using a constant ball position in your set-up, and I think you will see more consistent shots.

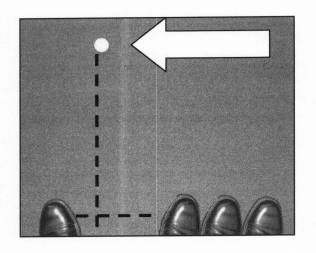

Constant position.

Many great golfers use a constant ball position, just inside the left heel, only moving the right foot wider, to accommodate the longer clubs. This is easier to learn, and generally produces more consistency for recreational golfers, and should be used for all shots from a flat lie. Measure the gap from your heels, not your toes.

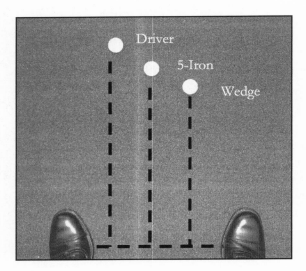

Changing position.

The alternative approach is to change the ball position progressively to the right, as the clubs get shorter, helping to create a more descending angle of attack, with the mid irons and wedges. Many better players will mix both methods, to better control trajectory, and ball flight.

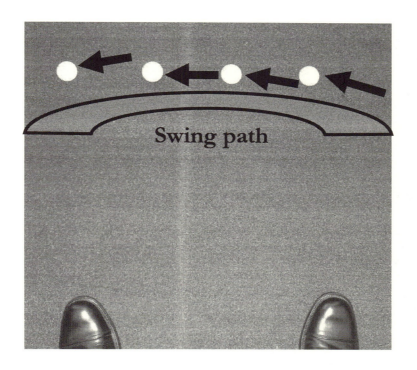

Swing path

Common faults.

If the ball is too far left (or forwards), in your stance, your shoulders will point left, causing you to cut across the ball, and slice. Should you play the ball too far back, your shoulders will be forced to point to the right of your target, usually causing a hook shot.

Get your ball position checked out, and you could play better next time.

Back to basics.

At the start of every new season, professional golfers will visit their coach, to check the fundamentals of their set-up, and so should you. Professional golfers understand that, 95% of poor shots begin with mistakes in the set-up. Frequently, when I am watching recreational golfers, they will hit what they thought was a "bad" shot, when they actually made a good swing, and did exactly what they set up to do. If you set up incorrectly, you actually need to make a bad swing, to hit a good shot. With a good set-up, good swings are rewarded with a good shot, and that will encourage you to make more good swings. This creates a positive feedback "loop", which encourages better golf. Also, by setting up correctly, you at least give yourself the best opportunity to hit a good shot. You have control over how you set up, so copy the pros and get it right. I cannot overstate the importance of the set-up in golf. So, if you really want to play better golf, make a commitment now, to re-visit each element of a good set-up at least twice a year.

It's complicated.

Although the client may not be aware of it, the golf teacher will frequently be juggling many variables, when advising on the fundamentals of grip, aim, alignment, ball position, and posture. This is for three key reasons:

1. Each set-up element is defined by your body shape, structure, and musculature.

2. Each element affects all of the other elements (e.g. change the posture and that will change the ball position).

3. Your power source is ideally created, as a result of your body type and shape. The set-up fundamentals need to change to fit with the power source.

So, although you can check your fundamentals with the information in the last few pages, you may find that you would benefit from getting a check-up from a competent and knowledgeable golf teaching professional.

Swing tips and tricks.

Do you know your correct power source?

You wouldn't expect everyone to wear the same shoe size, so why would you expect every "body" to swing in the same way? A well-trained golf teacher will endeavour to match the correct golf swing to your body shape; this will allow you to access your correct power source naturally. Identifying and understanding power source is a process I call "Body Type Analysis". I assess every client I work with, but will only share the information with those few clients who like that level of detail. The important thing is that you get to know how you need to swing to match your individual body shape, build, height, strength and flexibility. Get it wrong and it's like wearing the incorrect shoe size. Your swing will be powerless and uncomfortable. Get it right and you could unleash the swing you deserve. If you suspect you have a power miss-match, you could benefit from a check-up now.

Body type analysis.

In very simple terms, most people are one of three shapes. Short, wide and strong with limited flexibility, or tall, skinny, relatively weak, with considerable flexibility. In between these two distinct body shapes lies the medium balanced "average" body shape. Very few people fit exactly into a particular category. For example golfer, John Daly is incredibly flexible for his shape. Many older players would be tall and skinny, but with poor flexibility. My task in assessing a client, is to match the correct swing elements, to his, or her individual body type. Very few golfers will fit their swing correctly by chance - it requires specialist knowledge.

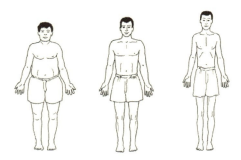

The thin and flexible body.

Here I am demonstrating the use of gravity, and a large circle, to compensate for a lack of bulk, and physical strength. Typically, the golfer will stand "tall" in posture, and swing the club in a high, and wide, circle to create the largest possible arc. Notice how my hands are considerably above my head in the back swing.

The young, thin, Tiger Woods and Nick Faldo, would achieve exactly this position, when they first played as professionals. From this position, a strong leg drive will assist the pull of gravity, to create a whipping action, to an elegant and high finish. Good timing is essential, to maintaining good ball striking, for this swing type.

USPGA Tour player Davis Love III is another example of this power source.

The big and strong body.

Because of the comparative lack of flexibility, this swing uses lateral motion to move the bodyweight away, and towards the target. Generally, the hands are kept lower to the ground, and considerable strength is used, to "chase" the club down the target line.

Many players with this power source, will take a large divot, and hit the ball with a left to right flight.

Some examples of players with this action would be, Craig and Kevin Stadler, Lee Trevino, and the great Arnold Palmer.

The balanced body.

This action is most common in the modern Tour professional. Using the bigger muscles of the trunk and thighs, to rotate around a centre point, balanced over "quiet" legs, the body can rotate quickly. This action then uses the set and release of the wrists to create mechanical advantage (or leverage) to generate apparently effortless clubhead speed.

Notable examples of this action would be England's Luke Donald, Steve Elkington and to some degree, most other Tour players.

This action is the most athletic of the three power sources and the most efficient, but does rely on the player maintaining the correct swing angles to keep the clubface on target.

Plane to see.

Almost every time you see a golf programme or read a magazine there is a reference to swing plane, but what does it mean and why is it so important? Well, the plane of the swing is simply the "natural" path your arms and the club will take around your body to collide with the ball. It's a bit like a door swinging on its hinges to fit back into the doorframe. If the door is off its hinges it won't fit easily back in the frame. Golf teachers assess swing plane by looking at the swing side-on and drawing a line from the ball through and beyond the shoulder socket. An on-plane swing will position the hands on this line at the completion of the back swing. If the swing deviates from the natural plane the club will need to be pushed or forced into the correct position to strike the ball squarely. The swing then becomes inconsistent and unstable, leading to all types of bad shots. You can immediately improve your ball striking by at least ensuring that your club and hands stay within the "safety zone", the triangle between the shaft line and your ideal swing plane. There are many other things to understand about plane, but I find this is a good way to get started. Check your swing, its plane to see.

The "Safety Zone".

Keep your hands and club swinging within this triangle and you should be more consistent. Think of this zone as being your margin for error - as long as you stay inside you are much more likely to hit decent shots.

The plane line is an imaginary line that passes from the ball through my shoulder socket. To swing at the ball correctly, my hands will be on this line at the top of my backswing.

Here I am correctly on plane with my hands in a perfect position. This will be a good shot.

Now I can swing naturally back down and into the back of the ball. Being on plane allows the player to swing powerfully and still produce accurate shots.

In this example the swing is too "flat", as if I am trying to hit a ball suspended at waist height. This would be great if the ball was sitting in a bush, but it's not! With this swing, it's almost impossible to consistently hit good shots with the ball where it normally is - on the ground.

This swing is too steep. From this position you will take huge divots and hit weak shots to the right. Making a swing from here, I would run the risk of hitting my right shoe with the club.

Pivot for power.

One golf myth that has caused many recreational golfers to develop swing problems is "keep your head still". The correct advice should really be keep your head level, as many beginners bob up and down in the swing causing a combination of fat and thinned shots. Trying to keep your head still will inevitably cause poor weight transfer and a weak, powerless swing. You could even develop the classic "reverse pivot" swing error. To create speed and power in the golf swing, you must pivot your weight fully to your right in the back swing (for a right handed golfer) and to the left as you swing through. At five feet, eight inches, and over 50 years old, I can still hit the ball as far as I could, when I was 20. This is because by creating a good pivot and swinging in balance, I can get the most from my swing. Follow these tips to improve your pivot and you could tap into your hidden power as well.

The reverse pivot.

In the picture to the left, the hips have slid to the players right and the spine tilts to the left. The opposite will happen in the downswing, leaking power and usually causing a slice.

A good pivot.

In the swing sequence above, the white line does not move; it shows the position of my spine. Notice how well balanced the swing is, and how I rotate around my spine, to allow the thickness of my chest, to move to the right, and left during the swing. This action is driven from the ground up, and leads the golf club, like a car pulling a caravan (particularly in the downswing).

A good pivot allows you to use the ground to create speed, rotation, and balance. Improve your pivot, and swing from the ground up, and you could find your distance, and power.

Incidentally, this drive carried 270 yards in the air.

The helicopter drill.

If you struggle with power or balance, try this drill, to feel a good body action and natural pivot.

Stand with your arms out, and moving through your feet, turn to your right. Make sure that all of your weight is on your right foot; turn your head as well during the drill (this will encourage you to turn your chest fully). Now move all your weight backwards onto your left foot, and then quickly turn, to finish in balance, with your knees touching. Notice how I have not used my arms to "swing"; they have remained quite still relative, to the rest of my body.

Practice this move frequently, and then try to incorporate the feeling of movement and pivot, into your golf swing, for every club.

How to hit the high shot.

All golfers will eventually be faced with a situation where they need to hit a particular club on a higher than normal trajectory, usually to get over a tree or similar obstacle while maintaining their distance. In addition, great golfers choose to control their trajectory (particularly for iron shots) as it is much more reliable than trying to control backspin. For example, if you are faced with a shot where your 8-iron is too little, but a 7-iron may fly over the green, hitting a higher 7-iron, will take off just enough distance, to drop the ball on the flag. Follow these simple steps and, with a little practice - you too will be able to hit the high ball when you want.

Hitting the "high ball".

My normal 7-iron shot.

Looking from left to right. In the first frame you can see my weight is evenly balanced between my feet, and the ball is positioned just opposite my heart, with my hands just ahead. In the second frame, I am fully coiled into my right side, with my back facing the target. In the third frame, just after impact, my weight is fully into my left side and the club is extending down the target line, stretching my right arm. During impact I maintained the original shaft angle; video analysis shows I am launching the ball at 16 degrees to carry 170 yards. In the last frame, you can see my left hand below my right, indicating a full, balanced release. Nice shot.

The high shot.

Hitting a high shot starts with the set-up. This is the same club, but in the first shot notice how around 80% of my weight is on my right and the ball is just inside my left heel. This change causes the shaft to angle slightly backwards, adding loft. The set-up has a more "up hill" look in the second frame, compared to the normal shot. Through frame three this allows me to maintain the original shaft angle and loft, sending the ball up at 27 degrees for 165 yards. Looking at the final frame, notice that my weight has hung back on my right foot slightly, and the extra active release of the club is indicated by more of my left hand being visible under my right.

Playing the low ball.

Golfing in Ireland, we are often faced with the need to keep the ball low and "under the wind". Although this shot can be used in the wind, the following technique is more effective for keeping the ball under low hanging branches and playing long, running shots from the rough and poor lies. With a little practice, you will have the confidence to position the ball well to your right, and then drive down and through, catching the ball first – and ripping it low.

Keeping the shot, low.

Playing the "low runner".

Using a 7-iron, I have positioned the ball just inside my right heel, with my chest ahead and my hands opposite my left thigh, reducing the loft on the clubface. I start with 70% of my weight on my left foot and I am careful to maintain that balance in the backswing. This creates a shorter, narrower backswing that will strike the ball more steeply; which is beneficial in the rough or in a bad lie. In frame three, notice how my chest and hands are well ahead of the ball and I have recreated the original shaft angle to control the trajectory. The back of my left hand continues to face the target in the next frame, and the reduced release is evidenced in the last frame, as you cannot see my left hand below my right. This shot launched at just nine degrees, and never got above head height, but ran to 175 yards.   An advanced version of this shot can be a real "stroke saver", when the width of your backswing or follow through is restricted by some obstacle. In that situation I have frequently taken a pitching wedge and positioned the ball *outside my right foot,* with my hands opposite my left pocket (de-lofting my pitching wedge to about a 7-iron). From that position I can use my wrists to pick the club up and chop down almost vertically into the ground, taking a huge divot with almost no follow through. Provided you contact the back of the ball first, the shot will come out low and fast and run for miles.

Hitting draws and fades.

Every golfer will eventually encounter a situation, where it would be beneficial to be able to manoeuvre a shot around some obstacle, for example a tree. Deliberately moving the ball in the air, from left to right or right to left, is quite straightforward, provided that you have a relatively sound golf swing. If you are one of millions of golfers who accidentally bend the ball in the air on every shot, then reading this section may help you understand what is going on.

Better players want to be able to "work" the ball, for several reasons:

1. It is much harder to hit a ball consistently straight; having a shape to your shots will improve your scores.

2. A shaped shot will create a bigger target. For example, a player hitting a fade (left to right) into a 40-yard fairway, can aim down the left side of the fairway and move the shot to the right, into a 40-yard target. A player aiming at the centre of the same fairway and attempting to hit a straight shot, can only miss by 20 yards (left or right).

3. Good players will try and aim their iron shots at the centre of the green and draw the ball towards the flag (if the flag is on the left side of the green). If they are unsuccessful in drawing the shot, then the ball will just "miss straight" and finish in the centre of the green.

4. Hitting a draw will usually cause the ball to fly half a club further whereas, a fade will fly a little higher and the shot will be half a club shorter. So, if you are facing a shot where an eight iron is too much but a nine is not enough, you could choose to fade an eight or draw a nine iron to achieve the correct distance.

5. Sometimes you just need to get around something that is in the way.

6. Working the ball is FUN!

I hear you ask, "That's all well and good, but how do I deliberately hit a draw or fade?" The simple answer is - provided you set-up correctly, it can be easy.

Setting up to hit draws and fades.

With a decent swing and a well-struck shot, the ball will start close to the direction that your clubface was aiming, and then change direction because of any sidespin applied to the ball. A ball with clockwise spin will move to the right and visa-versa. Sidespin is caused by the difference between the aim of the clubface at impact and the swing path (which is usually parallel to where your body was aimed). So to hit a fade, I will set up with the clubface aimed slightly left of the flag and my body aimed further left. Then all I need to do is swing normally. The swing path will pull the clubface *slightly* left through impact, causing the ball to spin to the right. The bigger the differential between the clubface aim and the swing path, the more the ball will bend. In the pictures below, first I am set up to hit a fade (left picture), then a straight shot and then a draw. Notice in the draw and fade pictures, how my body aim is different and the clubface is aimed <u>between</u> my body aim and where I want the ball to finish. All three of these eight-iron shots took a different route but finished within three feet of the flag.

Aiming the clubface.

To hit a draw, the clubface must aim to the left of your bodyline at setup, and impact - the opposite is true for a fade. Many players make the mistake of just twisting their hands until the club is looking in the correct direction. This will not work. Because of the forces created during the swing, your hands will just twist back to their original position at impact, usually causing the shot to just go straight. To successfully aim the clubface, you must turn the club in your hands to point the face in the correct direction, and then re-grip the club. At this point many players will dislike how the club feels in their hands, as any grip change takes time to become familiar. When you have changed the aim correctly then raise the club to hip height, and compare it to the pictures below. As before, on the left I am set-up to hit a fade, the centre picture is the straight shot and the last picture is for a draw. Once your set-up is correct, you must trust it. Then you can concentrate on making a good swing and allow the club to turn the ball through the air, exactly as you intended.

Hitting the shot.

In any well-struck golf shot, the first half of the ball flight is the result of the aim of the clubface, and then the differential with the club path will create the sidespin. In most swings the club will naturally follow a path that is parallel to the line of the body, although it is possible to force the club to swing on a different path, by overusing the arms. When trying to manoeuvre the ball flight, many players (even the top professionals), will set-up correctly and then inadvertently swing their arms and the club towards the target, rather than along their bodyline. As a result the ball will start towards the flag, and then move away. So the shot that should start at the left of the green and cut to the centre, actually starts at the centre and cuts to the right. To avoid this problem, you must ensure that you swing along your bodyline. Look at the two pictures below. They are both from real swings (a fade on the left and a draw on the right) and taken at the halfway point in my backswing. Notice how the shaft of the club is parallel to my aim line, showing that I am swinging on my bodyline and not at the end target. The club will also pass through exactly the same position on the downswing. Match this position in your swing and you could soon be having fun hitting draws and fades, just like me.

The downhill shot.

Playing from sloping lies is relatively easy as long as you get the basics right. First, for a downhill shot the slope will reduce the effective loft of the club and (because you are above the green) the ball will stay in the air longer. As a result you may gain up to 30 yards in distance, depending on the severity of the slope and change in elevation. You must accept that the ball will fly lower, but that is fine because you are above the green and the elevation will help to stop the ball. So in this example I played a 7-iron shot with a 9-iron. Second, play with the slope, don't fight it, and third, keep in balance. Follow these tips and sloping lies will add fun, not fear to your golf game.

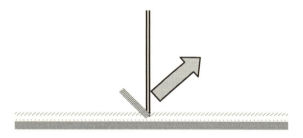

My normal 9-iron shot from a flat lie will usually fly 135 yards.

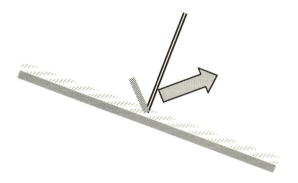

The same club played from this downhill slope could carry 155 yards because of the reduced launch angle.

75

First, the wrong way.

Here I am deliberately demonstrating a common error of trying to hit the ball "up" when playing from a downhill slope.

In the first picture you will see my weight is clearly on my right foot with my spine angled away from the slope. By the next frame, the setup causes my centre to get too far behind the ball, aiming the low spot of my swing at the high ground behind the ball. In the third frame, you can clearly see I have stayed on my right side in an attempt to get under the ball and, as a result, I struck the ground first. I tried my best here but actually missed the ball completely.

The bad setup gave me no chance to hit a good shot.

The correct way.

With the correct set-up, playing a downhill shot is easy.

In the first frame, I have set my weight on my left foot with my hips parallel to the slope. The ball is positioned slightly further to my right than normal, as the ground to my right is higher. In the second frame, I have swung around my centre keeping my weight more left than usual. I try and feel that I am "level" with the slope, and in the third frame this has allowed me to follow the slope with the clubhead, striking the ball cleanly. In the final frame, notice how well balanced I am. Set up and balance is key to playing from sloping lies; here you can see I have worked with the slope rather than fighting it. Excellent shot.

The uphill shot.

Playing the uphill shot is a relatively easy shot, provided you understand what is required. First, for an uphill shot the slope will increase the effective loft of the club and (because you are below the green) the ball will stay in the air for less time. So in the example, I played a 7-iron shot with a 5-iron. Second, play with the slope, don't fight it and third, keep in balance. In theory, uphill shots should be easy for many recreational golfers because the slope helps the ball to get in the air. However, I find that many players struggle because their poor weight transfer, during the swing, results in getting "stuck" on their right side (for a right handed player) and even falling away from the ball. The result is a ball struck with the club rising or even missed altogether and that is no fun at all!

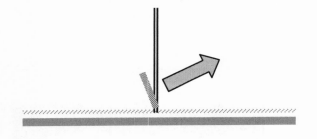

My normal 5-iron shot from a flat lie will usually fly 185 yards.

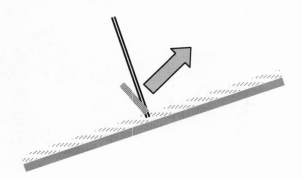

The same club played from this uphill slope could carry 155 yards because of the increased launch angle.

First, the wrong way.

Here I am deliberately demonstrating a common error by chopping down on the ball, when playing from an uphill lie.

Look carefully at the first frame, and you will see that my weight is clearly on my left foot, with my spine angled into the slope. By the next frame, the setup causes my centre to get too far ahead of the ball, aiming the low spot of my swing, at the high ground to my right. In the third frame, you can clearly see I have stayed on my left side and the club is falling steeply to the ground. At impact, my weight is too far ahead of the ball, causing a deep divot and a low weak shot.

The setup caused the hill to get in the way.

The correct way.

With the correct set-up playing the uphill shot is easy.

In the first picture, I have set my weight on my right foot with my hips parallel to the slope. I like to keep the ball position around about the same as a regular shot, or slightly further to my right. In the second picture, I have swung around my centre keeping my weight more right than usual. As with a downhill shot, I try and feel that I am "level" with the slope throughout the swing. In the third picture it is clear I have followed the slope with the clubhead, striking the ball cleanly with my weight moving to my left. In the final picture, notice how well balanced I am.

With the correct set up it is easy to swing with the slope, letting the club do the work, while I stay in balance. Nicely done.

Playing shots from slopes.

Many recreational golfers struggle with this shot because they try and fight the natural ball flight created by the hill. By understanding the effect of playing from a slope and planning for it in the shot, you can ensure a better result. Try this. Hold your pitching wedge in front of you with the head at eye level and the leading edge vertical. Now can you see where the loft of the face is looking? Somewhere over your left shoulder (if you are right handed) so, if you had to hit a ball at eye level with a 52 degree pitching wedge, you would probably need to aim at least 52 degrees to the right to hit the target! Understanding the effect of the slope and making an allowance in your set-up can solve most of your problems. Follow the tips below and you could play like a pro from the next sloping lie.

A ball struck correctly from a level lie will fly straight, at right angles to the leading edge of the clubface. When playing from a slope, the club lie naturally changes the aim of the clubface, and the ball will follow the slope, as shown in these pictures. Change your aim to allow for the effect of the slope.

Set-up for sloping lies.

With all shots from sloping lies, you must alter your set-up to compensate for the slope and the change to the ball flight the slope will cause. Try and fight the slope and you will lose.

Changing your set-up to match the slope.

Look at the three different lies I have set up to in the pictures below, and you will clearly see how I have changed my aim, posture and distance from the ball to fit the shot. Looking from left to right, in the first picture the ball is three inches above my feet, in the second it is almost level, and in the third, it is three inches below.

Playing from a level lie.

For reference, here I am playing from a flat lie to the sixteenth green at Woodstock Golf Club, Co. Clare, Ireland.

In the first picture you can see that the line through my body is parallel left of the target (circled), and the clubface is looking directly at the flag. Halfway through my backswing the shaft is pointed at the ball, putting my swing on the correct plane. At impact the club is swinging parallel to my bodyline, sending the ball directly towards my intended target. In the final picture, because I have swung in balance I can hold this position until the ball lands.

Playing a ball above your feet.

Prepare correctly, and you can master this shot.

Compare each picture to those on the previous page. Key to playing this shot well, is understanding that the ball will "follow" the slope by moving from right to left in the air, flying a little further than usual. One good strategy is to use one club more than usual and swing a little softer. In the first picture, see how far right of the (circled) target I am aiming; the actual ball flight is shown moving the ball 50 yards in the air. Notice also that I have shortened the club with my grip; my weight is towards my toes and my posture more upright. Maintaining my posture, in the second picture, I have flattened my swing slightly to keep the shaft pointing at the ball. Through impact my body is a little quieter than usual with my weight still towards my toes, and I have made sure that the swing follows my bodyline, starting the ball correctly to the right of the green. In the final picture, it is clear that this was a balanced and controlled swing, leaving an easy birdie putt.

Playing a shot with the ball below my feet.

To reach the ball I am more tipped over and a little closer than usual; also I am aiming 30 yards left of the target, to allow for the left to right shot caused by the slope. In frame two, notice how I have maintained my posture and created a slightly steeper swing by keeping the shaft pointed at the ball; I like to feel that I dip my left shoulder slightly at this point. At the top of my backswing (frame three), my hands are slightly higher than normal with my left arm pointing directly at the ball.

Compare my head position (relative to the tree line) for these pictures and you will see they are identical, evidence that my posture remains the same throughout the swing. If your posture changes during this shot, you will almost certainly "top" the ball.

The downswing.

From the correct position at the top of my backswing, I can now drop my arms and the club down the "slot", powerfully into the back of the ball. In the second frame you can see the ball (circled) starting exactly where I am aiming. The ball will fly with a gentle left to right flight, landing near to the flag. In the final frame, I have maintained my original spine angle and allowed the club to swing through impact freely, pulling my right shoulder under my chin, to a balanced finish.

Sloping lies can be fun - it's the truth.

Playing in the wind.

Tom Watson (one of the greatest bad weather players of all time) advised, "When playing in the wind – take two more clubs and chip it around." I agree. Over 40 years ago, I learned to play golf when I lived in St. Andrews (the home of golf) and there are few better places to develop a good wind game. Here are a few tips on how to play on wild days. First, remember that the weather is the same for everyone; it's easy to slip into thinking that you are the only person suffering. Second, you can't change the laws of physics; a 30 mph head wind will reduce a good drive by 80 yards, but playing down wind you only gain 30 yards, make allowances. Third, "hit it low" is not always the answer. Great wind players can reduce the spin they create (below that of a normal shot) and consistently control the trajectory of each shot. Fourth, enjoy the challenge; it's what golf is all about. I hope this lesson helps your wind play.

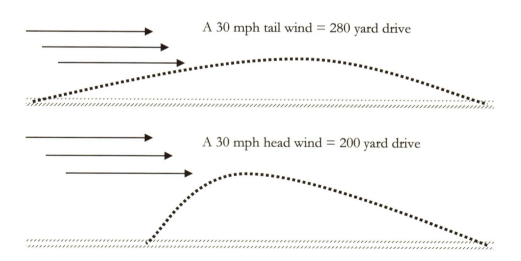

A 30 mph tail wind = 280 yard drive

A 30 mph head wind = 200 yard drive

1. In this example I am playing a 140-yard shot (normally a 9-iron) with a 7-iron. I am going to hit the ball 9-iron distance with a 7-iron trajectory and the spin of a 5 iron. To help achieve this I will turn my 7-iron into a 9-iron by going down the grip, until it is the same length as my 9-iron.

2. In my set-up I have positioned the ball as I would for a 9-iron shot, with the ball the same distance away. During the swing I want to keep my chest over the ball like a 9-iron shot and not slip into playing a 7-iron, in fact I make an extra effort to "think 9-iron".

3. I reduce the amount of wrist employed and therefore the spin created by gripping a little tighter and firming up my arms. It is important not to rush the swing and ensure you make a full backswing with your shoulders.

4. Through impact I concentrate on "sweeping" the ball away (rather than digging or scooping the shot). This is my finish position; notice the extension in my arms and the club pointing at the sky. Perfect.

Swing drills.

Drill your swing change in five easy steps.

Did you ever see Nick Faldo practicing with a beach ball between his knees, or Harrington with a glove trapped under his armpit? Using swing drills is the easiest and quickest approach to correct your swing errors. This is because drills help you to "feel" the change, rather than having to think about it. Tour professionals generally prefer to work with swing drills when trying to groove a change, because they like the simplicity and the ability to revisit the feeling (even during competition). Often commentators suggest that drills are "too technical", but the exact opposite is true. Like me, many good golf teaching professionals devise swing drills to make teaching easier, and to let the player focus on the new feeling, rather than trying to remember a head full of body movements and club positions.

Over the next few pages, I will share some of my favourite swing drills. I hope you will try them out. But beware! Many golfers make the mistake of thinking that they can make changes to improve their golf swing by just hitting a few practice shots. Then they are disappointed (and embarrassed) when the change doesn't work on the course immediately. They decide that the change must be wrong and discard it, until the next golf lesson, or idea from some armchair expert on the television. Even the world's best golfers have to have confidence in their swing changes before they play (and so should you).

Follow these five simple steps to apply and consolidate changes and you will succeed. Be honest and patient and remember it is OK to go back a step, or all the way to step one if you need to at any time.

Step one.

Learn and practice the technique or swing action *without* a ball. Use mirrors and video to help you develop the correct action and discover the feeling that you will look to repeat later. This is a most important step.

Step two.

Apply the new swing or action to a golf ball. Don't worry particularly where it goes; focus on checking that you reproduce exactly what you did in step one. If you find that the swing changes when a ball is present, go back to step one and practice some more.

Step three.

Now try and apply the swing to a ball and a target. Can you repeat the new swing and find a target? Can you consistently predict where the ball will go? If not go back to step two or even step one and continue to build trust in the new action.

Step four.

Apply the new swing to a golf course - try it out on your own at first and don't be afraid to try the same shot two or three times, to build confidence. Use step one as practice swings, to help consolidate the feeling you want to repeat.

Step five.

When you feel ready, apply your new swing to a scorecard, and then in competition. Start off gently with reasonable expectations, and above all be kind to yourself. Don't get mad, if you hit a poor shot. Change is a building process.

1 – Release your inner golfer and cure that slice.

Many golfers who slice or hit the ball excessively from left to right (for a right-handed golfer), do so because they have an over-active body action or grip the club too tightly. The result is the handle of the club returning to the ball before the clubhead – causing the clubface to look to the right of the target. When the ball is struck with the clubface "open" to the target line the ball will spin clockwise, turning from left to right in the air.

The "Feet Together" drill is designed to provide the feeling of allowing the clubhead to catch up with the handle and pass the body through impact. Follow the steps below and you could cure your slice. Other benefits of using this drill are improved clubhead speed and better balance.

Step one.

Place the ball on a low tee and select a 9-iron. Do not attempt to hit to a flag at this stage, just look for an improved ball flight in the direction you are aiming. Stand with both feet together, directly opposite the ball. Take care to maintain a slight flex in your knees throughout the swing.

Step two.

Keeping a light grip swing back allowing your wrist to set fully. Keep your body still and your weight centred between your feet. You should "feel" as though your knees, hips and chest are still facing the ball and you are just swinging your arms and the club. Keep your arms and hands relaxed.

Step three.

Stay balanced and let the club swing down and through hitting the ball with a slight right to left flight. Watch through impact to see the clubhead swing past your hands. Maintain your balance (until the ball lands) with your knees and hips facing the front. You should feel that your arms have wrapped around your chest.

Step four.

Practice the drill regularly both with and without a ball. Then try hitting balls with your feet apart but maintain the same feeling of a "quiet" body and watching the clubhead passing your hands through impact.

When you play, make a few practice swings with your feet together to remind yourself of the feeling you want to achieve on your shots, then when you hit your shots you can concentrate on the correct feeling. Many golfers like this approach as it also occupies their minds with a single positive "swing thought".

Changes can take a long time to consolidate, but drills can speed you along.

Drill your swing number two – throw it all away!

Many recreational golfers swing with a very poor body action. This upsets the natural sequence of legs, body, arms then club that is common in good swings. Poor body action is the cause of many swing errors. Some people will hook shots because a slow body action causes the clubhead to pass the hands too early in the swing, sending the ball on a looping flight to the left. Others will slice because they attempt to compensate for a lack of power by pulling the club to the left – across the intended swing path.

Good body action and sequence is essential if you want to consistently strike the ball well and far. This "step" drill is excellent for helping golfers to feel the correct body movement because it is a natural motion that is easy and quick to learn. When most people throw a ball (right handed) they load their weight on their right foot, then they step towards the target, load their weight into their left and twist their hips before firing the right side to throw the ball. Compare the ball throw with the drill and swing series pictures and you will see that the body action is pretty similar. If you can learn to throw a ball, then the step drill is easy.

Make practice swings first, then try hitting golf tees and eventually put a ball on the tee (don't worry too much about where it goes, just focus the correct body action). You will be amazed by how effortless your swing will feel as the ball rockets into the distance. Finally, hit shots by keeping your feet in place but still move your weight in the same sequence, just like you are throwing the club away.

Go on and try it, just throw it all away!

Step one.

First, practice throwing a ball with your children, or your dog, or skip some stones across a lake. Take notice of how your weight naturally moves away from the target to begin with, and then leads the arm, moving into your left, before you throw. A bad body action would throw the ball at the ground (where your golf ball would normally be positioned), whereas good body action would allow you to throw the ball horizontally 30 to 50 yards to your left.

Step two.

Set up to hit a 9-iron with the ball on a tee. Now pull your left foot to your right, keeping your weight on your right foot as you swing the club up. Then replace your left foot to its original position and drive your weight into your left. Once your weight is fully committed to the left, you will feel that your arms and the club will be pulled down. Now (and only now) you can swing through the ball, as if you were attempting to throw the club towards the target. Hold your finish position until the ball lands.

Step three.

Hit 10 decent shots with the previous step drill before you try the same action without taking an actual step. You should try and feel the same sequence in your swing, in particular the downswing being delayed until your weight is fully into your left side, and your arms and the club are being pulled down naturally.

Always hold your finish until the ball lands. On the course, you can use the step drill to refresh the feeling of a good body action and the correct swing sequence.

Thumbs up for better ball striking.

I find that many recreational golfers strike the ball very poorly, and lack the sort of effortless clubhead speed that is evident in the swings of better players. One reason is that, in trying to hit the ball further, they grip the club so firmly that their forearms and wrists lock solid. This encourages the hands to travel too fast through impact, and causes the clubhead to travel slower, almost at the same speed as the hands. This action gives the illusion of speed and power because of the effort it takes, but actually produces the opposite result. Video and computer analysis of top players shows that their hands actually _slow down_ through impact, allowing the speed to be transferred to the clubhead, so in the better swings the clubhead travels considerably faster than the hands through impact. That is the difference between the professional's effortless power and the club golfer's powerless effort.

Arms locked solid in an attempt to hit the ball a long way!

Drill three – the "thumbs up" drill.

This drill is excellent for helping you feel the correct hinging of the wrists at either end of the golf swing. Many golfers who try this action for the first time are immediately struck by how lightly they need to grip the club. Grip too firmly and the clubhead cannot freewheel through impact and you will be unable to point your "thumbs up". As with all swing drills, first try the new action without a ball, to understand and consolidate the feeling. Then try and include the feeling in a swing, without really worrying about where the ball is going (obviously only try this where you have plenty of space.). Only take it to the course when you have mastered the new action. You may find that this drill (or another) does not work for you. There are hundreds of swing drills and dozens of ways to learn a new element of the swing. Part of the skill of the teaching professional is identifying which swing drill is best suited to you and your swing. Owning a spanner doesn't make you a plumber – sometimes you need to consult a professional. Give me a call – I will be happy to see you.

Thumbs up!

Step one.

If possible, start this drill facing a mirror or window, where you can see your reflection, and still have enough room to swing a golf club. Take your normal posture while facing the mirror, without a club. Make a half swing back until your left arm is horizontal and your thumbs are pointed at the sky. Check that the back of your left hand is facing the mirror and your weight is on your right instep. Now swing down and through to a point where your thumbs are again pointing at the sky and your weight is firmly on your left foot. Look at the mirror to check you can now see the back of your right hand. Repeat the action frequently, taking notice of how your forearms rotate smoothly as they pass your centre.

Step two.

Once you feel comfortable with the action, repeat step one with a 9-iron swinging your
arms slowly to a horizontal position or "thumbs up". Notice how the clubhead swings
considerably faster than your hands. Make sure you still transfer your weight correctly,
grip the club lightly and allow your forearms to rotate. Once you are confident you
have mastered the action, go to the practice ground or a quiet area of your course, and
try hitting a few shots. Tee the ball up at first and begin with half swings, until you get
used to timing the new action. Eventually you can swing the club to a full backswing.
This action is common to all full shots from sand-wedge to the driver. Be patient and
have fun.

Swing drill four – get connected for better consistency.

If you have ever pushed a supermarket trolley with a "wobbly wheel", then you can already appreciate the negative effects of disconnection. We often hear that a chain is only as strong as its weakest link; well the golf swing is very much a chain reaction, where disconnecting one link can break the chain and ruin your swing. One common error I find with many recreational golfers is a disconnection of the arms from the body. This is when the upper arms separate from the chest and operate separately to the trunk (see picture). This can cause any number of swing errors that change from day to day and even from swing to swing, something that many players would describe as being inconsistent.

Good golf swings flow from the ground up, through the body to the club and then the ball. Each link in the chain of events follows the one before in a natural sequence that stores, then releases energy, very efficiently. To work consistently, each link in that chain must stay "connected" to the links on either side. Break the link and the swing will falter. For example, it will come as no surprise to discover that breaking the chain, by letting go of the club, will cause you to miss a lot of shots. I see a lot of disconnection errors in recreational players. Young players tend to over use their legs and hips creating a disconnection from the upper torso, the result is a slice and a sore back. Conversely, stronger players are inclined to lock their legs and over use the chest and arms in an effort to "muscle" the club through impact. Then, because the body has stopped, the left arm will disconnect in an effort to keep the club moving, causing shanks and hooks.

Disconnection.

By far the most common fault is a disconnection of both of the arms from the body, usually caused by trying to swing in a fashion that exceeds your flexibility. When the chain is broken the arms are no longer "synchronised" with the body and a random selection of horrid golf shots occur. The "towel drill" is a favourite practice drill of many top professional players and teachers, as it quickly re-establishes the connection between the arms and chest. Once the connection is made, most golfers find that the rest of the swing links up in the correct sequence. Remember, swing drills are there to help you identify the correct feeling of the change you want in your swing. Follow the steps below to practice the towel drill and you could quickly improve your consistency. Go on – get connected!

The "Towel Drill".

Only practice this drill with a 7-iron to pitching wedge. Get a hand towel, roll it into a tube and place it under your upper arms and across your chest. Make a few gentle practice swings, but do not allow the towel to fall out. You may notice that your swing will feel considerably shorter than usual. Most golfers immediately feel a need to move their weigh far better, from foot to foot, and pivot more. This is fine, as long as you can stay in balance. Look at the swing sequence, and you will see how my weight moves significantly from side to side, but always **from the feet up.** Once you are comfortable with the new feeling, try hitting some soft pitching wedge shots, with the ball on a tee. If the towel falls out, then you are disconnecting. Eventually you can work up to hitting full shots with a 7-iron, again while staying connected. Discard the towel and try some shots with the longer clubs, but maintain the feeling of "pressure" under your armpits and you should be able to maintain connection. If you lose the feeling, go back to using the towel. Once you have mastered the new feeling, you can take the swing change to the course, but please – not immediately in competition! Stay connected and I am sure that you will see an improvement in your consistency.

Swing drill five – plane and simple!

Swing plane may be one of the most important factors in the golf swing. You can get away with quite a few swing errors if you have a good swing plane, but you will need to have excellent body motion, sequence and timing to hit any good shots at all, if you are swinging "off plane". In a good swing, the club and your arms swing on an extended line from the ball through your shoulder socket (when viewed "down the line"). This allows your arms to swing the club naturally back to the ball. Any deviation from plane would miss the ball completely, unless the club is forced into a different path with the hands. This drill is a favourite with many professionals as it is easy to use, gives quick results and allows you to hit balls immediately. I have hit thousands of shots with this drill; it's a simple way to find your plane.

On plane!

The pre-set drill.

Provided that you pay attention to the detail in the set-up, this drill will get you hitting shots from a perfect, "on plane" position, almost by the first swing. Lay a shaft on your toe line, aimed at the flag, but extending away from the target. Place the ball on a low tee peg and (using no more than a 7-iron) set up ready to hit. To start, cock your wrists and rotate your arms away from the target, until the club shaft is parallel with the ground in a toe up position, and directly over the shaft that is on the ground. Ensure that your hands are still opposite their original position and no further away from your body. Check your position against the two pictures above.

Downswing.

Now, without changing your wrist-set simply
turn your shoulders until your left shoulder
points to the right of the ball (for a right
handed player). Your weight should be 80% on
your right foot. From this position, all you need
to do is uncoil through to your finish position,
collecting the ball on the way. Hold your finish
in balance until the ball lands. Notice how the
"on plane" swing causes the club to pass
through a pre-impact position that is the same
position as your pre-set. Perfect.

Swing drill six – a handy drill.

Many swing errors occur, or begin, because of an incorrect use of the non-target side of the body (the right for a right-handed player or left if you play left-handed). Although I like to think of golf as being a two-sided game, I do accept that the strongest side of your body will be inclined to dominate the swing, and consequently cause more swing problems than the leading side. Many teachers and players try to correct errors by making the left side (for a right-handed player) work harder. Although this can help, I have achieved quicker and more lasting results by training the dominant side to do its job correctly.

Try the "one hand drill". Even if you don't have a swing problem, it may improve your game. As with all drills, try it first without a ball, then with a ball on a tee, then after you have hit 10 good shots, hit one with both hands on the club while maintaining the feeling of a one-handed swing.

On the course make one-handed practice swings to refresh the feeling.

The one-handed drill.

The benefit of this drill is that, unless you are immensely strong, it is almost impossible to consistently hit good shots one-handed, if you make bad swings. So, if you hit a good shot, you must have made a good swing! Take your normal set-up with a pitching-wedge, and the ball on a tee. Remove your target side hand and gently grip the bicep of the other arm just above the elbow joint, maintain your grip throughout the swing. Make a normal backswing; check that your right forearm (for a right handed player) is parallel to the line of your spine when you reach the top of your backswing.

The one-handed drill – downswing.

As you swing down (see the first picture above), allow the club to "fall", rather than pushing it, so that the shaft points at the ball. This position is key, as the club can now naturally swing into the back of the ball. In the next picture, notice how the rotation of my body has kept the butt of the club pointed at my belt buckle. This position is common to all good ball strikers. You may hit the ball as hard as you like, provided that you can strike every shot well and hold a balanced finish. Ensure your grip pressure is light enough that your wrist remains flexible, but your hand stays in contact with the grip throughout the swing.

Swing drill seven – get a running start.

Many recreational golfers, struggle to make a suitably wide and full turn, and therefore lack power in their shots. This is particularly true of those who are getting older, lacking flexibility, or players who are physically large through the chest. I frequently see golfers like that, who struggle to achieve the distance and power, which someone of their height and strength is capable of. Inevitably, the problem can be traced back to a poor turn and a lack of lateral weight shift. This swing drill can also be used for most regular shots, to help fix the problem in one easy step. I have been using this idea since I first saw the extravagant Canadian Tour professional "Moe" Norman, who always set up with the clubhead several inches behind the ball, in an effort to improve his width and turn. Moe is generally recognised as being the most accurate ball striker in the world – ever. If you lack power, you may wish to try a running start.

Former Canadian Tour player Moe Norman with the clubhead several inches behind the ball at address.

The "Running Start".

Start in your normal set-up position. Initially you should use a 7-iron with the ball on a low tee peg, but you can quickly progress to hitting normal shots with any club. Next, move the clubhead to a position just outside your right foot, and two inches inside the ball target line. Rest the clubhead on the ground and pause for three seconds. Look at the picture above and you will see that my weight has moved into my right side and that my shoulder line has changed to a slightly "closed" position. This will help you to make a better turn.

Downswing.

At the top of the backswing the "running start" has helped me move well into my right, with the line through my shoulders pointing outside my right shoe. The downswing is initiated by a deliberate shift of the hips towards the target; the result is a slight "squatting motion" that pulls the club down and through. Just before impact I am aware of fully committing my weight to my left side and releasing the club freely through the ball. Take the feeling (of the running start) to the course - it worked for Moe.

Swing drill eight – "It don't mean a thing if it ain't got that swing." (An old song title)

The golf swing is called a "golf swing" because good golfers really do swing the club and just let the ball get in the way. This principle is fundamental to being able to create a good golf game. When the focus changes from making swings, to trying to hit at the ball, there is an immediate (and detrimental) change, to how the body moves. There's a lot more biomechanics and physics involved here than most people want to know about.

Over 50 years ago the great golf teacher, Jimmy Ballard, created the phrase, "Make the dog wag the tail, don't let the tail try and wag the dog", to encapsulate the concept of just swinging the club; it's such a good analogy, that it has been used by teachers ever since.

This is the first swing drill I ever invented, and I have been using it regularly for over 30 years. Since then, I have discovered many top teachers have also developed their own version. We all use this drill because it quickly imparts the feeling of swinging the club, and (because of the physics and biomechanics involved) the body starts to move correctly almost immediately.

Try my "Swing/Swing drill", and you could stop playing like a dog and start swinging like a pro.

Repeat 10 times

The Swing/Swing drill – just swing like a child's swing.

Start by preparing a ball on a tee ready to hit, it is best to begin with a 7-iron, but any club is suitable, as long as you appreciate that we are looking for a swing feeling – so accuracy is (initially) not expected. Stand a few feet away from the ball, parallel to the intended target line. Make a practice swing through to a full finish, with all your weight on your left foot (for a right handed player) and hold that position. Now step your weight onto your right foot and *swing* to a full backswing position. Just before you reach the top of your backswing, move onto your left foot and *swing* through to a full finish position. As soon as you get to the finish, step back onto your right foot and swing back again. Continue to swing back and through 10 times without stopping. Make the swings smooth, easy and fluid, ensuring that you move your weight **before** you move the club.

The swing.

Once you have the feeling of swinging freely, stop, and step forward so the ball is in the way. Then make another **swing,** through to a balanced finish. As the ball gets in the way of the swinging club, you will be delighted how it rockets away, with effortless power. Repeat the drill frequently, until the swing with the ball, feels exactly the same as the swing without it. Take it to the course, by making swing/swings three or four times, just before you play a shot, to remind yourself of the correct feeling, particularly just before you hit your driver.

Swing drill nine – the one-handed "Whip it" drill – part one.

This is an excellent drill, to help your game if you lack distance or slice, as both problems can be caused by poor hand action, restricting the correct release of the clubhead.

Get your driver and turn it around, so the head is at the top and the handle is near the ground. Take your normal grip on the shaft, just below the head, then remove your left hand and put it behind your back. Now make some full golf swings, using just your right hand, through to a full finish. Make sure that you don't hit the ground, as you may damage the club. Try and "whip" the club through, so the handle makes a loud "whoosh", as it passes your left foot. You will notice that you will create more speed (and whoosh) when you soften your wrists.

The one-handed "Whip it" drill – part two.

Next, put both hands on the club and make the handle make the same sound, as it did when you used only your right hand. Finally, turn the club around and swing normally. Because you are desensitised to the weight of the club, you will feel the clubhead pull you through impact. Perhaps, for the first time ever, you can now feel what it feels like to release the club correctly.

Once you master this drill, you can try hitting shots. Most people are delighted by how far they hit the first ball, but find they have to revisit the drill, to keep the feeling fresh.

Go on – whip your game into shape.

Swing drill 10 – the power wedge.

One of the little known, but essential power indicators, that I look for when conducting video analysis, with one of my clients, is the hip position at impact. There is a direct relationship between the hip position, and how far the player hits the ball. Over the years, I have come to notice that, in the impact positions of the longest hitters, the belt buckle and fly zipper will reach the position of a line drawn, from the outside of the left hip to ankle, at set-up. This is only visible on high-speed video and computer analysis, as in the example below. This power wedge drill is proven to improve the hip position at impact, and increase power, and could probably increase your distance, even if you have not had your swing professionally analysed. Give it a try – you could just hit it further.

The "power wedge" drill.

For this drill, you will need a pitching wedge, a 7-iron and a few golf balls. Place your pitching wedge face down on the ground, so that the leading edge is at right angles to your intended target line, and the club is where you will put your right foot (for a right handed player). The intention is for the back of your wedge, to sit under the outside of your right foot, so it tips the foot towards the target. From that position, swing away with your 7-iron. At the top of your backswing, your right knee should retain its original flex, and you should be conscious of your weight pushing into your right instep.

The "power wedge" drill – the downswing.

Once you have the feeling of pressure on the inside of your right foot, at the top of your backswing, you can "push" smoothly into your left side, leading with the hips, and swinging the club powerfully through impact. At the end of the swing, all the weight should be on your left foot, with your right shoe up on its toe. This drill is excellent, for creating the feeling of resistance in the right side in the backswing, and a powerful move towards the target, with the body leading the club, into impact. Hit five good shots with this drill, and then try one shot without standing on your wedge, but look for that same feeling of resistance in your backswing. Repeat this drill frequently, for a permanent power improvement.

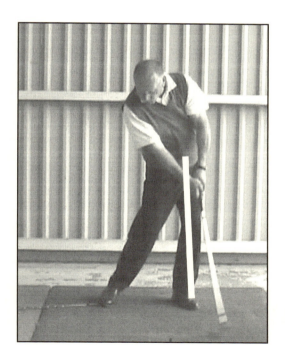 

The Short Game

Putting

Putting basics.

As with everything in golf, developing good fundamentals in putting can help tremendously, in improving your consistency and scoring. It is true that, because the forces involved in the putting stroke are substantially less than those of a full swing; you can vary from the ideal, and still putt very well. We must never forget that the ultimate intent of the putting stroke is to get the ball into the hole. That is why so many tour professionals experiment with different putter models and designs, in the hope of an improvement. I am sure that many tour professionals would gladly wear a pink tutu and stand on one leg, if it was proved to make them putt better! (It doesn't). However, the basics of the putting stroke are well known and understood, so if you start out by following the tips on the next few pages, you will give yourself the best opportunity of developing an excellent putting stroke.

The putting grip.

One key to excellent putting, is a grip that makes it almost impossible to flick the clubhead. A common mistake made by recreational players, is to grip the putter as you would your driver, as this will encourage unwanted wrist action in your putting stroke. The grip employed by the majority of better players is the "reverse overlapping grip". In this grip (which you can use for chip and run shots as well) the club lays diagonally across the palm of the left hand, following the line of the index finger, to just below the muscle of the thumb. The last three fingers of the left hand will only touch the grip with the pad, as if you were playing a flute. The left index finger rests lightly, along the outside, of the middle joints of the right fingers. On a scale of one to 10 (with 10 being the strongest), your grip pressure should be no more than three. I do not encourage players to put the right index finger down the side of the grip as, when you putt under pressure, it is inclined to twitch unpredictably.

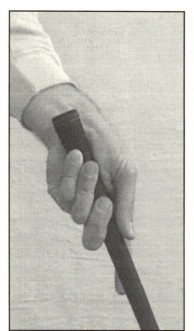
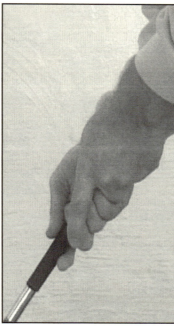
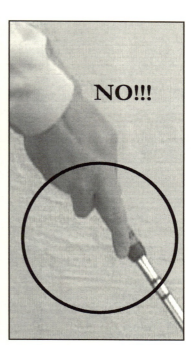

NO!!!

Putting set-up and stroke.

However you putt, you must do the following – if you are going to roll the ball well, consistently and on line. At setup, the putter face should look exactly where you want the ball to start its roll. At impact the putter face should pass through the same setup position, travelling on the intended line, with the clubhead rising slightly and travelling at a constant speed. The shaft angle at impact should replicate the setup exactly, or the loft on the putter face will have changed. The putter must not turn, twist, descend or decelerate through impact.

In your setup, keep your eyes over the ball-target line, with your hands below your shoulder sockets, and your upper back level. Viewed from in front, your sternum and eyes should be two inches behind the ball. This set-up will encourage a slight upwards stroke through impact, helping the ball roll end-over-end. In your putting stroke, try and use more shoulders than arms and hands, and control your distance by changing the length of your stroke, rather than by how hard you strike the ball. Your through-stroke should be slightly longer than the backswing and you should hold the finish position until the ball stops rolling.

"Y" the pros putt so well.

All great putters maintain the angles, created at address, throughout the putting stroke. Looking from the front, the arms and club, create a letter "Y", with the putter being the tail of the "Y". This keeps the putter face looking at the target, and allows you to control your stroke by simply "rocking" your shoulders. Any change in putter shaft angle, between set-up and impact, will cause the putt to miss – either by changing the aim, ball speed, clubface angle, or all three. Even some of the top tour players, struggle with this breakdown from time to time. It is the reason why so many professionals now putt with "belly putters", which lock the top of the putter into the middle of the torso. This then acts as a pivot point, keeping the arms and chest connected. Once you have mastered keeping your "Y" throughout the putt, you can control your distance and speed, by the length of your stroke, and not by how hard you hit the ball. The result will be improved lag putts, and much more consistent pressure putting. Now you can see "Y" the pros putt better than recreational players.

The wrong way.

In the picture on the left, I am demonstrating the typical error of collapsing the left wrist and breaking the "Y". This is a common fault with many recreational players. It could be described as hinging the wrists, or hitting with the hands. Whatever it is called, the "Y" has broken down, causing this putt misses on the left.

In these pictures, you can clearly see that I have maintained the angles set at address, and will hold my finish position until the ball falls in the hole. Looking from left to right at the pictures above; you can see that the letter "Y" created at address is unchanged throughout. The handle of my putter continues to point at the centre of my torso. My feet, legs and hips, remain very still during the stroke. I like to imagine that I am standing on a chair and need to keep my balance, so I don't fall off. My head only turns after the ball has gone. I hold the putter lightly, and just rock my shoulders. This is a great putt.

Wedge perfect putting.

Many club golfers make the mistake of striking their putts with a descending blow that creates backspin. The ball will then skip and bounce, several times, before it starts to roll correctly. This causes inconsistent distance control, and putts that fail to stay on the intended line.

One of the most effective practice drills, to encourage a good putting stroke, is to try putting with your sand-wedge. Follow the set-up and grip on the next page, and putt away. If you strike your putt with a downward stroke, the ball will pop up in the air. A good stroke will produce an excellent "roll".

Most pros can putt almost as well with a wedge, as they can with a putter. Give it a try. It may improve your putting, and it will come in handy should you ever forget your putter!

Here is a real example of what happens when a putt is struck with a descending blow. This was a 20-foot putt. Look at the shadow of the ball, and you can clearly see the ball is almost two inches in the air! That would be good for a chip shot, but not helpful for your putting consistency.

The wedge putt drill.

For this drill, I am using my sand-wedge to putt. In the first sequence, I am demonstrating the effect of a "high to low stroke". When using a wedge to practice putting, any downwards motion will cause the leading edge of the club to get under the ball, creating a chip shot.

Obviously, here the ball has popped up into the air. Not a good stroke.

Here, you can see the wedge has swung from "low to high", so the leading edge of the club has struck the mid-line of the ball - setting it rolling, with immediate topspin. In the backstroke, try and feel that the club almost brushes the grass, and only rises just before the ball.

A putt with this stroke will roll consistently, and hold its line on even the bumpiest of greens.

Great stroke.

Good putting – it's routine.

The best way to cope with the pressure of putting is to make the unfamiliar, familiar. You can do this, by sticking to the same routine for every putt. Top golfers have a putting routine that is so consistent, that you could time it with a stopwatch. Many recreational players have no real routine, or even worse, they have a routine, but change it when the putt seems important. Here are the six steps, which I feel are essential, to any good putting routine. Do this on every putt for a month, and you will never want to change. I guarantee it.

Great putters have a routine.

1. Read the putt.

I always look from behind the ball and, if in doubt, behind the hole. I try to walk beside the line of the putt, to feel the slope in my feet. Don't second-guess; the first impression is usually right.

2. See the putt.

Jack Nicklaus called it, "going to the movies". Picture the putt rolling along the green, at the correct speed, and falling into the hole. Try and feel like you have already seen the real putt go in.

3. Feel the stroke.

Make some practice strokes, while looking at the target (not the ball). Make strokes until you are positive that you feel the correct stroke, to create the putt you have just imagined.

4. Commit to the stroke.

Many players fail at this stage. You must truly believe that the stroke you have visualised is correct.

The wrong putt, played well, is much better than the right one, played badly.

5. Repeat the stroke.

Now, this is actually the easy bit! All you have to do is aim, and repeat, exactly, the stroke you have committed to use. Don't doubt yourself. Try and feel that this is the tenth time you have played (and made) this putt.

6. Hold your finish.

All great putters do this. Hold the finish position, and focus your eyes on a spot just behind the ball. Avoid the temptation to "take a peek". Inside 10 feet, just listen for the ball to go in the hole.

Use a line to align.

Have you ever noticed the line that many professionals have on their golf ball, and wondered what it's for? Well here is the answer. First, the line is OK, and legal for competitions, because you are permitted to mark your ball for identification. So you can draw the line, using a CD pen, or, if you prefer, many ball manufacturers preprint a line on the ball. For a professional, the line serves two purposes – to show that the ball has been struck correctly, and to help create the correct aim. When a ball is rolled correctly, "end-over-end" with a putter, then the line will be visible, as the ball rolls. But the line will wobble, or disappear, when the ball is poorly struck.

An incorrectly struck ball will leave the clubface with sidespin and excessive backspin, that will cause the ball to roll inconsistently, causing more missed putts. This usually occurs, when the ball is not struck with the "sweet spot" on the putter face, or when the strike is not parallel to the target line. Second, research shows that most golfers aim incorrectly when putting, and actually have to mishit putts for the ball to go in the hole. A high percentage of professional golfers, now use a line on the ball, to help them aim correctly, particularly from inside 10 feet. They can then focus on making a pure stroke, which sets the ball rolling on the intended target line.

Some of golf's greatest putters freely admit that, at the moment of striking the putt, they do not care if the ball goes in the hole. This is because, at that point, they are only concerned with making a good stroke, which will set the ball rolling, end-over-end on the correct line. This would amaze most club golfers, as they can think of nothing else but trying to get the ball in the hole. Perhaps your putting would improve, if you could aim correctly.

Try the line to align.

Correct your aim.

This bit is harder than you may think, and it takes a little practice, before you try it in competition. However, it is far easier to point a line in the correct direction, standing behind the ball, than it is to aim your clubface, while standing over the ball! When setting your aim, you need to point the line at your intended start line; this is not necessarily the hole. In the picture your line would be aimed 30" to the right of the hole, to allow for the slope, then gravity will turn the ball into the cup, (this is called the "read"). The intension is to make every putt a straight putt, allowing gravity to do the rest. Through experience, your read will gradually improve, but I can give you a little help. Most people under-read their putts by a considerable amount; initially you will be safe to triple your read, so if you think you need to aim 3" to the right then aim 9". This may seem excessive, but trust me, and give it a try. At worst you will miss the putt on the high side where the ball still has some chance of falling in.

Perfect your stroke.

Many golfers, even professionals, regularly mishit their putts, which will result in inconsistent direction, and poor distance control. Indeed, golfing history is littered with examples of championships being lost, because of a poor putt on the 72nd hole.

Creating a stroke that can produce a smooth, "end over end roll", is far easier if you practice without a hole to putt to, simply try and roll the ball about six feet. Place the ball with the line on top, then align the line on your putter with this line, and finally place your body at right angles to the putter shaft. Now make a stroke, which follows the extended line away and through the ball. If you strike the ball correctly, the ball will roll so the line is visible and solid. Any mishit will make the ball wobble as it rolls. Keep practicing, until you can create a perfect roll every time, then try putting to a hole, and see if you can still roll it like a professional.

Go on – give it a try.

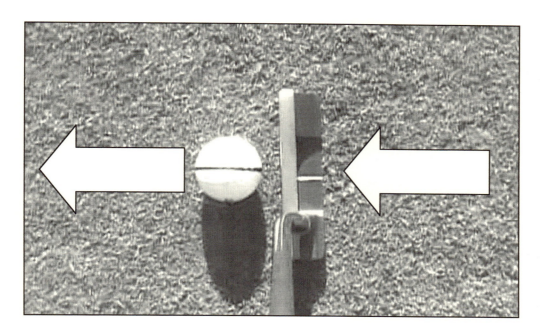

Use the toe to keep it slow.

Short downhill putts, on fast greens, can be frightening. The problem is that you need to make a soft enough stroke to stop the ball racing by the hole, but firm enough to keep the ball on line. A trick many top golfers use, is to strike the ball from closer to the toe of the putter. This reduces the energy transferred to the ball, giving a "dead" feel to the strike, slowing the putt, but keeping it on line. As with any new technique, you must practice before you use it for real. Never try a shot in competition, which you haven't played successfully in practice, at least 10 times.

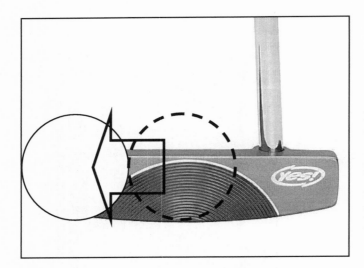

Have a few practice strokes, with the intention of making a short, but firm, stroke. Then take your usual putting set-up, and aim. When you feel comfortable, move both feet backwards one and a half inches. Now set up with the ball towards the toe of the putter.

This is a simple and easy stroke to master, with a little practice. By striking the ball with the toe end of the putter face, much less energy is transferred into the ball. This will permit a shorter, firmer, more positive stroke. Trying to hit a fast putt normally will usually result in a decelerating stroke, which causes the ball to wonder off target. A more positive stroke, will keep the ball on line.

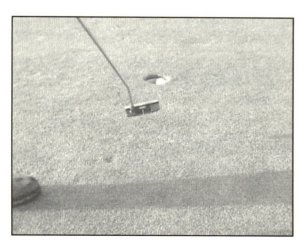

Make sure that you keep your stroke on line, and strike the ball near the toe of your putter. Many people inadvertently swing the putter away from the body, and strike in the middle of the putter. You must make an extra effort to swing the putter on the intended line, striking firmly, with the toe end of the putter.

149

With a little practice, you can use the same idea to kill the speed on those tricky downhill chip shots. I have frequently seen recreational golfers play this shot by accident, leaving the ball short of the hole. Use the same principles in your set-up, as you would for the putt above. Make a firm downwards stroke, striking the ball towards the toe of the club.

From deep rough, the pros will also try and strike the ball high on the face, and near the toe. This will create a very soft shot from a firm swing. As always, practice before you try this in competition.

Chipping

Perfect chipping made easy.

Many recreational golfers are doomed to hit horrible chip shots, before they even move the club. This is because, they incorrectly think that the clubhead needs to get under the ball, and lift it up, and this causes them to hang back on their right foot, while "scooping" the club with the right hand. When the clubhead passes the hands in the chipping stroke, it travels too fast, and rises from the ground. As a result, your chip shots will either pop up too high, or scoot along the ground - like a startled rabbit. Inconsistent contact and club speed, will also ruin any chance, for predictable distance control.

Great chipping starts with the correct set-up, und understanding how to control club speed, and shaft angle. Follow these tips, and you could be on your way to better chipping.

In this example you can see my weight is on my right foot, and the clubhead has "flipped" past my hands.

The clubhead is leaving the ground, and turning left. A good chip shot, with this technique, would be pure luck.

Please study this great chipping sequence carefully. Looking from left to right. In the set-up, notice how I am square to the target line, with my weight left, and hands ahead of the ball. In the second frame, my weight stays left. Between frames two and four, look at how far my hands have travelled. It is far easier to control distance with a small amount of wrist hinge, and a "long" hand travel, as this reduces shaft speed. Through impact, I keep the clubhead low, keeping the heavy part of the club, *below* the centre of the ball. Finally, in frame three, notice how the shaft exactly matches the original angle, maintaining the intended trajectory. Perfect.

The two ball chipping drill.

This is a great way to practice and develop good chipping technique.

Place two balls about five inches apart directly in line with your intended target. Use your highest lofted club (usually a sand-wedge). Set up with the front ball opposite your right instep and the second ball five inches to the right. Try and keep at least 90% of your weight on your left foot and your hands opposite your left leg. Now swing the clubhead to miss the second ball with a *downward stroke*, keeping your weight to the left. If you try and "scoop" the chip shot you will hit both balls by accident.

The secret of chipping under pressure.

Do you find that you can handle a simple chip shot, from a yard or so from the edge of the green, in normal circumstances, but under pressure, you "duff" it, or send the ball scooting across the green? Most likely, you are using too much wrist, allowing the clubhead to pass the handle, and causing the club either to strike the ground before the ball, or hit the ball half way up. It is generally and indication of a poor chipping technique, which you may get away with sometimes, but it will inevitably let you down when you least want it to. This is because under pressure, the small muscles of the wrist and hand are inclined to "twitch", and flick the club unpredictably. The same problem also occurs with putting, for many recreational golfers.

The solution was discovered by golf professionals, and applied to both putting and chipping, many years ago, I first noticed the great Jack Nicklaus chipping with this method, almost 35 years ago, when I lived in St. Andrews.

Basically, all you need to do is putt the ball with a 7 iron, using a putting grip and stroke. The only change is to position the ball below your right eye, (if you play right handed), so that the club meets the ball while descending, rather than ascending, as it should for a putt. Then all you need to do is make a stroke of the correct length, using just your arms and shoulders, and the ball will pop onto the green, and roll to the hole. Avoid trying to "chip" the ball, or make it go up. Just think putt, and let the loft on the clubface do the work of getting the ball to jump the fringe grass.

It is a simple and effective method – try it, and I guarantee you will love it.

Set-up and stroke.

In the first picture, you can see that my weight is balanced, with 60% on my left foot. The ball is just opposite my right instep, and the shaft of the club, is tilted slightly left, keeping my hands ahead of the ball. Look at my head relative to the background in all three pictures, and it is clear that the only things moving are my arms, shoulders, and the club. If your set-up is correct, then all you need to do to make a correct stroke is, rock your shoulders. A good way to master this method, is to practice putting to a target from the fringe, with the ball opposite your left heel, so you strike it on the way up. Then change to a 7-iron and position the ball opposite your right heel, so you strike it on the way down. Use the same stroke and grip, as you did with the putt, and the ball should hop onto the green and then run across to the hole, the same distance as your putt. Concentrate on staying still, and using just your arms and shoulders, to make a stroke that is of equal length, on either side of the ball. With a little practice, you could soon have a pressure proof chipping action.

Think "four", for a better score.

I find that many recreational golfers are very one-dimensional, when it comes to playing shots from around the green. In most cases, they automatically reach for the pitching-wedge, regardless of the shot they are facing. When I ask why they chose that club, the usual response is, "Isn't the pitching-wedge supposed to be for pitching?" The answer is - not any more! "Pitching-wedge", is the original name for the club, but the club has changed. We call our woods by that name, because they were originally made of wood. They are now mostly made of titanium, but the original name sticks.

Pitching-wedges, used to have a loft of 52 degrees, but the modern sets (in an effort to hit the ball further), have pitching-wedges with lofts of as little as 44 degrees, which was once an 8-iron. No wonder golfers struggle to get the ball into the air. I encourage my clients to get creative when chipping, and consider four options, before choosing the club that will give them the best chance to save a shot.

Try it yourself – you may improve also.

8-iron and pitching wedge lofts over time.

	1960's	1970's	1980's	1990's	2000's
8-iron	44°	43°	40°	38°	34°
PW	52°	51°	48°	46°	44°

The chipping challenge.

This is a fairly typical example, of the "chipping challenge" most golfers will face, more than ten times in a round of golf. Your ball has run through the green, and is lying a couple of yards from the putting surface; you need to get "up and down", to save your par.

First look at the lie. Can you putt the ball through the fringe? On average, a poor putt will do better than a poor chip. If you can't putt, then can you chip the ball over the fringe, with a 7-iron, and allow the ball to run to the hole like a putt? If there is not enough room, or perhaps you are playing down hill, consider playing with a 9-iron, to throw the ball a little further and create less run. Finally, if you have discounted all the other options, then use your sand-wedge to throw the ball around 70% of the distance, and let it check at the hole.

Don't confuse creativity, with being reckless. Good golfers have a flexible approach to chipping, which lets them choose the shot, which is *most likely* to produce the best result. Consider these four options each time you face a chip shot, and you may cut your handicap by more than half.

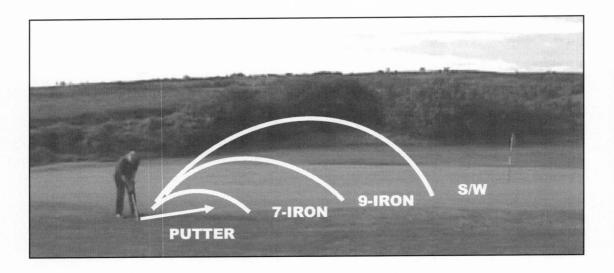

Bag it – winter chipping practice.

This is a great chipping drill, because it teaches good technique, and you can't cheat. Many golfers try and "scoop" their chip shots by swinging the clubhead from low to high (trying to hit the ball on the way up). If you scoop the ball in this drill, your ball will hit the golf bag, and finish back at your feet. Position your golf bag one metre away from the ball, and at right angles to your bodyline. Don't worry about a target; your job here is to get the ball over the bag. Make little swings, where the clubhead swings from high to low, try and feel like you are going to hit your bag, with the club. Finish low, and the ball will go high, finish high, and the ball will go low, and into the bag. Practice this drill this winter, perfect your technique, and bag it for next season.

Here I am demonstrating the incorrect technique.

The clubhead finishes high, and the angle in my left wrist has changed. With the ball positioned left of centre, the club strikes on the way up, sending the ball into the bag. A chip played like this, would shoot right across the green.

The correct way.

Using your sand-wedge, set up with the ball just inside your right heel. Position your hands inside your left heel; the shaft should lean towards the target. Position your golf bag about one pace (or metre), away from the ball.

Your weight should favour your left foot.

Notice in this picture how my hands have only moved around 60 centimetres, but the clubhead has swung past the level of the handle. This action is key in getting the clubhead to swing high. If you allow your hands to travel too far, you will be unable to swing the clubhead up.

Low

Here you can see, that my weight is on my left foot, the clubhead is low, and the angle in my left wrist, is identical to the set-up. Notice that because the clubhead is low, the ball (circled) is high. This shot will land softly and stop quickly.

The chop and stop.

This is a handy little shot saver, to have in your repertoire. You won't need it every time you play, but when you do use it, your friends will say, "Wow! How did you do that?" In this situation, your ball is just off the green, and sitting deep into the roots of thick, lush, rough. You need to get the ball out, up, and stop it quickly. The problem is – swing hard enough to get the ball out, and you will hit it too far, swing softer and the club will snag in the rough, and only move the ball a few inches. The solution is the "chop and stop" shot, where you swing hard enough to get the club through the rough, then use the ground to take off the excess speed at impact. When the club stops, and the ball will jump up, with very little energy, to land softly on the green. With a little practice, you can look like a magician, and escape from an impossible position.

Here I have set up, with the ball positioned opposite my right toe, and the handle of my sand-wedge is pointed at my right pocket. My left hand is turned a little further to the right, so I can see four knuckles. This will help to create a bigger wrist set, in the backswing.

In this frame - notice that my hands have only moved a few inches, but the clubhead is level with my chin. I am using a lot of wrist here. However, you must resist the urge to flick your wrists on the downswing. Although you can't see the ball yet, believe me – it is in there.

This is a great picture. See how my hands are well ahead of the clubhead and, compared to the first image, I have increased the shaft lean. As a result, the clubhead has fallen steeply, into the back of the ball, and then the ground, with a thump.

Notice here, how the clubhead has stopped its forward motion, and actually bounced upwards. Do not think that the club stops here because I decelerated – quite the opposite is true. Because I used the ground to slow the club, I can swing harder. I concentrate on holding the angle in my right wrist, and allowing the club to stop naturally. The ball (circled) has popped up softly, creating another great escape.

The high lob shot.

This is the shot, that most recreational golfers want to be able to hit, but can't. However, most professional golfers can play it, but don't (unless they have no other option). The reasons are simple.

1. It's a difficult shot to play well, and requires a lot of practice, to consistently achieve a better result, than any alternative shots.

2. The ball needs to be "sat up" slightly, so the club can slide cleanly under the ball.

3. You need the correct equipment - many tour professionals will carry a lob wedge, with a loft of up to 64-degrees, but most club golfers only have a 55-degree sand-wedge.

4. Although a well-played lob shot can get you out of a fix (because of the clubhead speed required to throw the ball sky high), a mishit will usually fly 80 yards, into an even worse position.

So my advice to most golfers is: - chip out sideways, and hope to make a long putt, or buy a 64-degree wedge, and leave your 3-iron in the garage.

If you still want to learn to play the high lob shot, here's how. But remember; even the world's best will only play this shot after lots of regular practice, and when there are no other options.

Understanding what you need to do with the club, is important to playing this shot well. Many club golfers, incorrectly attempt to "scoop the ball into the air, and end up either laying a divot over the ball, or hitting it across the green at knee height. When this shot is played correctly, the clubface is almost at right angles to the sky, and will graze the **underside** of the ball, at close to driver speed.

A good way to practice for this shot, is to put a ball on a tee, two centimetres from the ground, grip your sand-wedge with the face looking at the sky, and try and make swings that knock out the tee, without touching the ball. Remember, to develop the confidence and ability to play this shot, there is no substitute for practice.

Set-up and stroke.

In the first picture, notice that the ball is positioned one inch to the left, of the centre line between my heels, my body is aimed 45 degrees left of the flag, and the clubface is 45 degrees open (looking at the sky). You must open the clubface, then grip the club, don't just twist your hands. To minimise leg action for this shot, I like to add some additional knee flex, which I will maintain throughout the swing.

In the second picture, my head and hips have not moved, but I have turned my shoulders almost 90 degrees, with a full wrist set. I try and keep my eyes looking at a spot, two inches behind the ball, where I want the club to start to slide through the grass.

Notice in this picture, just how close the clubhead is to the ground. By keeping my head and hips still, I am able to swing the club wide and low, but fast enough to hit this 15 yard shot, 30 yards into the air.

In this final picture, you can see that I have kept my right hand under my left; this keeps the clubface looking at the sky. The shaft is pointing at my belt buckle, showing that I have not flipped the club, or attempted to scoop the ball.

Finally, see how the club has passed the ball. This is clear evidence that, although the club is travelling at considerable speed, the glancing blow created a high-flying shot, which landed like a butterfly, with sore feet!

Bunkers

The four levels of bunker play.

Before we look at the mechanics of playing bunker shots, I want to demonstrate the tactical thinking that is required to become and remain a good bunker player. Regardless of your ability, each bunker shot will present one of four possible shots:

1. Just find a way to get out of the bunker, even if you must putt out backwards.

2. Get out of the bunker and on the green, somewhere.

3. Get out of the bunker and close to the hole.

4. Get out of the bunker, onto the green, and into the hole.

Choosing the correct option every time is the sign of a great bunker player. Good golfers will choose wisely, based on the lie, sand and their ability and level of practice. Lesser players will frequently select the shot that exceeds their ability and luck! Next time choose wisely.

"Too much ambition, is a bad thing to have in a bunker"

Fun in the sand.

The scorecards, of many recreational golfers are doomed to a "sandy grave", every time they try to hit out of a bunker. This is because they totally misunderstand how the shot is played. Bunker shots are easy, because they are the only shots in golf, where you don't hit (or even play), the ball. You just play the sand. In the bunker shot, the back edge of the club sole, is used to skip the club through the sand, causing an explosion that throws sand, and the ball, out of the bunker. If you struggle with bunkers, try practicing swings in the bunker, without a ball, just skipping the sole of the club through the sand, and focusing on throwing the sand out. Once you have mastered that, then all you need to do, is practice the tips that follow, and you are on your way. Just like a day at the beach – have fun.

In this excellent high-speed photo, you can clearly see how my club has bounced through the sand, exploding the ball out. Notice how the club has passed the ball (arrowed), and the sand explosion, by some distance. Had I hit the ball, it would not be visible in this picture.

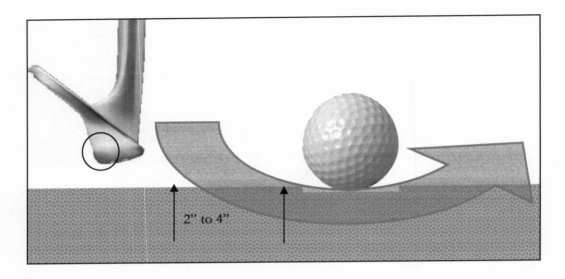

Bunker basics.

As you can see in this graphic, the back edge of the club sole (or "bounce"), is used to strike the sand, two to four inches before the ball. This will cause the club to pass under the ball, throwing an explosion of sand, and the ball, out.

By far the best practice for your bunker game - is to play sand shots without a ball. Draw a three by six inch rectangle in the sand, and make swings to throw the rectangle of sand, out of the bunker. When you can consistently throw the entire rectangle of sand, out of the bunker, then draw another rectangle, and place a ball in the centre. Ignore the ball, and concentrate on throwing the sand out, exactly as you did earlier. The ball will then fly out, on an explosion of sand – it's easy! Then, when you play bunker shots, imagine the back edge of your rectangle, and focus your eye on the area of sand you want to hit. All you have to do then, is throw the sand, and the ball, out onto the green.

Resist the urge to peek at the ball, when you play bunker shots, because, if you look at the ball during a bunker shot, you will miss the sand and hit the ball.

More bunker basics.

Set up to play a bunker shot, my body is aimed 30 degrees to the left of my target, but the clubface is looking at the flag. I am aiming to strike the sand, on a line between my heels, and the ball is two to four inches, to the left of that point. I have flexed my knees an extra inch, to help swing below the ball.

Bunker shots are best played with a long slow swing, which continues to accelerate to your finish. Here I am swinging the club back, along my aim line, and not on a line to the flag. Notice how I maintain the same knee flex throughout this shot. This is key to good bunker play.

In this picture, you can see the club has bounced through the sand, on my aim line, but the ball is flying towards the flag (this is on the line of the clubface), indicated by the blue arrow. Notice how "quiet" my knees and body are. This is very much an arm swing.

Pitching

Set your clock to control your distance.

65 – 75% of golf shots, in a round of golf, occur from within 100 yards of the green, with the majority being played with the wedges. I find that most recreational golfers, can hit their wedges fairly straight, but they have very poor distance control.

Professional golfers, understand the importance of the "scoring zone", and control distance by carrying up to four wedges, and applying three different length swings with each club. I like to control my swing length by imagining a clock face, and swinging my left arm to a particular "time". I always try and swing the same distance, on either side of the ball, so in my half swing, my left arm will travel from nine o'clock, to three o'clock. My full swing with a wedge goes from ten to two o'clock, and my quarter swing, from eight o'clock to four. It is quick, and easy, to learn three swing lengths, and once you build a little trust, your scoring should improve. Professional golfers learn their distances, and even keep them written on the shaft of each wedge. The effect of the "four by three wedge system", is equal to having, 12 wedges in your golf bag.

Most golfers would score much better, by carrying an additional wedge, and leaving a long iron in the garage. However, even if you just learn to control your distance, using the following clock face approach, I am sure you will save shots, from 100 yards.

In the following examples, I have shown the distances I hit my wedges, from different length swings. This is to demonstrate the range of shots you can develop, by using three swings for four clubs. It really doesn't matter, how far you hit your wedges, as long as you can predict each shot, by setting your clock.

Go on – try it!

Get more wedges.

About 20 years ago, the pitching wedge was 52°, the standard P/W today is 48°, but the sand-wedge is still 56°. To fill the gap, pros now carry a 52° "gap" wedge, and for higher shots, a lob wedge of 60 to 64°. Carrying more wedges, with equal gaps in the lofts, gives you much better opportunities to score, when close to the green.

Playing the wedge shot.

From a narrow stance, position the ball just inside your right heel, with the grip pointed towards your left hip. Keep your weight favouring your left foot. Make a smooth, unhurried swing, and ensure that the length of your follow through, matches your backswing. Aim to strike the ball, then turf, with a descending blow, that takes a shallow divot, around three inches long.

Rather than trying to force the shot, my key thought here, is to control my swing length, and allow the ball to fly its natural distance.

The benefit of knowing your wedge distances - is that you will be able to play more aggressively, to a tight flag position, in the sure knowledge that the ball **will definitely** clear that pond.

8 o'clock

By swinging my left arm to this **eight pm** position, I hit my four wedges to:

Pitching wedge 85 yards

Gap wedge 65 yards

Sand-wedge 50 yards

Lob wedge 40 yards.

9 o'clock

My **nine pm** swing will produce:

Pitching wedge 100 yards

Gap wedge 80 yards

Sand wedge 75 yards

Lob wedge 60 yards.

10 o'clock

A **10 pm** swing will fly the ball:

Pitching wedge 120 yards

Gap wedge 110 yards

Sand wedge 90 yards

Lob wedge 80 yards.

These are my in the air distances, not allowing for run, or backspin, and measured in dry and warm conditions. I use these distances as a benchmark, and will add or subtract some yards, to allow for conditions, and temperature. My wedges may have different lofts, and shaft lengths, to yours, and the ball I play may spin more (or less), than the model you use. ***Do not*** try and copy my numbers – you need to discover your own. I do this by hitting 10 balls, with each club and swing length, on an "average weather day", then measure, and take note of the distances. If possible hit your shots into a bunker, as the balls will not bounce or run, and you will be able to get more accurate carry distances.

Get passionate!

If your partner (or significant other) is a golfing widow, or widower, you would do well to have given a little gift for Valentine's Day to say, "Thank you for putting up with me and all my bad moods." You could also consider, trying to improve your golf scores, to help put a smile on your face, after each game. Top golfers love the scoring clubs (the wedges and putter), and they have real a passion for scoring. They delight in the challenges, presented by the golf course, and the opportunities to use their skills, to "steal" shots from the course. Great players are never happier, than when they practice, and play shots, around the green. If you can chip the ball dead, from a difficult lie, get up and down, from a deep bunker, two-putt from 60 feet, or hit a wedge shot stiff, to make birdie on a long par five, I guarantee you will smile more, after golf. Follow the tips and drills below, to get passionate about your scoring, and you may find that you need to buy fewer flowers and chocolates next Valentine's Day!

Some hard facts.

Most recreational golfers are unaware of some critical facts, about the short game Take a moment to consider the following. For any round of golf, at least 70% of shots are played from inside the "scoring zone" (less than 100 yards from the flag); this is the area where any improvement, can have the biggest impact. Even the best putters, on excellent greens, will miss 50% of putts from six feet, and 90% from outside 10 feet. To be 99% sure of making a putt, you need to chip the ball to less than 24 inches. To score better, you must putt or chip that approach shot closer.

A few tips for passionate scoring.

Make it fun. To improve, you must practice. Regardless of your technical faults, practice will improve your confidence, and consistency. Make your practice interesting, and fun by inventing games, and challenges. Try playing two balls and pretend you are playing against your favourite professional.

Stop three-putting. Many club golfers will have several three-putts in each game and incorrectly believe that they need to improve their short putts, when they actually just need to get their long putts closer. The fault is inconsistent lag putting. They have poor control over direction and speed, on long putts. Practice various long putts to an umbrella laid on the green. A ball that stops, against the umbrella, will be close enough to guarantee a two-putt.

10 short putts. Improve your pressure putting, by trying to make 10 consecutive putts, from 30 inches.

Pitching – control your distance. Most golfers have reasonable control of direction, on shots when pitching to the green, but have very poor distance control. Experiment with your sand-wedge, until you can consistently hit the ball three different distances by either controlling the length of the swing (easy), or how hard you swing, (harder to do). Try for 20, 40 and 60 yards, as they are the most common approach shots you will face.

Spot your chip shots. Practice chip shots that land the ball on a specific spot on the green, rather than trying to get the ball to the flag. Lay a towel on the putting surface, than try and make each shot land on the towel, on the first bounce. When you chip to a green, you can then visualise the "spot", you need to land the ball on, to run to the flag.

Bunkers – play the sand. Good bunker play is all about being able to play the sand and not the ball), as it is the sand, which throws the ball out of the bunker. If you understand that, where the sand lands is also where the ball will land. Then all you need to do is practice throwing the sand, where you want the ball to land. Use your sand-wedge to practice, throwing the sand to a target. If you can control the trajectory of the sand, then you will be able to do the same, with the ball. I recommend you practice so the sand stays in the bunker, otherwise the golf course will soon run out of sand. After a while introduce a ball, and aim two inches behind it, then focus on throwing the sand, where you want the ball to land.

Miss it smart. Many golfers guarantee a dropped shot (or worse), by missing the green in places, which would challenge even the best tour professionals. Before you play an approach shot, look at the green, and consider where you would have the easiest chip shot, or putt, if you were to miss the green. Usually this would be an uphill shot, with a decent area of green, to land the ball in. Try not to leave yourself a downhill, down wind shot, over a deep bunker.

Get a lesson. Most golfers would get tremendous value for money, if they took a short game lesson, and practiced what they learned. Typically, players will have some mechanical faults that, once fixed, will improve their consistency. But, there is also a huge amount to learn, about tactics, and how to play those, "shot savers".

Practice chipping to a towel.

Managing Your Mind.

The mental game of golf.

I find that many recreational golfers feel, that the mental side of golf is unimportant – something only for professionals, or people who can't cope with pressure. They could not be more wrong. The mental side of golf is at least 25% of the game and, on those occasions when your golf game is working flawlessly; managing your mind is really all you need to worry about. Learning how to control your thinking, and emotions, can have a substantial effect on how well, and consistently, you play golf. In any round, most golfers, even professionals, make more mental mistakes, than physical mistakes. It is far easier, quicker, and more profitable, to eliminate your mental mistakes. Over the next few pages, I will introduce some of the tips, and tricks, I use with both my professional, and amateur clients. Whether you are eight, or 80, male, or female – get serious about your mind management, and you could be a better golfer - by just dreaming about it.

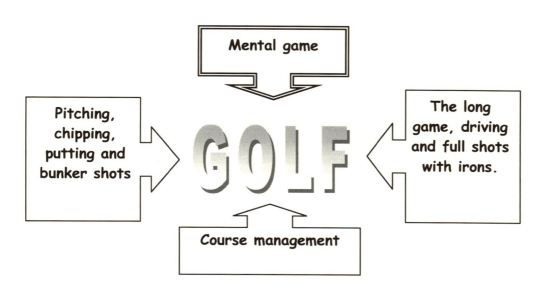

Get positive!

When I watch a client preparing to hit a shot, I will sometimes ask, "where are you aiming?" The answer is frequently something like, "not in the bunker (or trees, or water, etc)". Our minds are naturally good at maintaining positive thoughts, but an odd thing happens, when we try the negative approach. If you try and keep the thought "don't hit it in the water", half way through your downswing, I guarantee you will become more positive, and think, "HIT IT IN THE WATER"! And you will. The correct thing to do is to focus on what you want, and not on things that you don't want.

Pick a small, specific target, and picture only the thing you are trying to achieve, so your mind is only able to "see" the correct target. This is sometimes described as having, "tunnel vision" – where you are only able to see where you want to go. It's like driving a car, or riding a bicycle, where you look at where you want to go, and make the car go there, rather than thinking, "Miss the lorry, miss the trees" and so on. When you play, keep just one positive thought in your mind, rather than many negative thoughts.

Before you play each shot, check that you are positive!

The negative approach.

Here you can see into the mind, of many recreational golfers, just before they hit. This golfer, is trying to keep at least five swing thoughts in mind, all of them negative. It would be like, trying to juggle five hand grenades – drop just one, and you could ruin your entire day!

Also, focusing on the things you don't want, would mean that, in this case, you could only apply one fifth of your mental energy, to playing a good shot.

I recently played with a professional colleague, visiting from England. After he hit his opening tee shot, 10 yards *less* than the divot, he admitted that his swing thought was, "Where did I put my passport?"

Even the pros get it wrong sometimes!

Get positive!

Here you can see the target, through the eyes of the professional golfer. Although there are trees, water, and bunkers, which make the shot potentially disastrous, the player has only one thought – the target.

Personally, I find that I hit some of my best shots, when I am demonstrating; because, having described my intended shot to a client, I have a clear and simple picture, of the shot in my mind.

Next time you play - make an extra effort to:

- Create a clear picture, of the shot you want to hit.

- Pick a small, specific, target.

- Take dead aim.

- Focus on what you want.

Improving your confidence.

"An inability to forget is far more devastating than an inability to remember - in both golf and life".

The best way, to find the confidence to play a difficult shot, is to remember a previous occasion, when you have played a good shot, with that particular club. Visualise your best shot. Professional golfers, will have a bank of good shot memories to draw on, but most club golfers, just seem to have a head full of bad shot memories. Why is this? Most people would say, that it is because of all the bad shots, recreational golfers hit. Not true.

Professionals hit bad shots as well, lots of them. The difference is that, the pro has elected to create powerful and positive memories, from their good shots, and accept their bad shots, as something that happens to everyone. Recreational golfers however, frequently accept their good shots, as if they hit them all the time, but react to bad shots, with horror, and rage.

Emotions are key, in creating strong memories; most people, remember exactly where they were, when they heard about the atrocities on 9/11. This is because there was a strong, negative emotion, associated with the event. However, if you were lucky enough to have a big win on the Lotto, I guarantee you would also remember, where you were, when you first read the numbers!

So in future, remember your good shots, with passion and pride – and set them in stone. Accept your bad shots, with quiet dignity, and forget them as you would, an unused telephone number. Develop a selective memory. Remember the good, and forget the bad, then you too, will have a head full of good shot memories, which you can bank on.

Keep a bank of your good shots and remember them with passion and pride.

The mental game of golf.

If you didn't know how good you were, how good would you be? For most golfers, the answer is, "A lot better". This is because, much of what they do on the golf course, lacks real commitment, and therefore causes a crisis of confidence, resulting in a poorly played shot. Words like confidence, and commitment, are common in television golf coverage, but why is it so important? Well, imagine you are doing a freefall parachute jump, today. You decided to pack your own parachute, but only with 50% **commitment.** Now, how **confident** are you, that your jump will be successful? However, if today was your fiftieth jump, and you knew both your main, and reserve parachutes, were packed correctly; then your confidence level would be much higher. Golf presents similar challenges. Getting the most from your golf (regardless of ability) requires a good understanding, of how to maximise confidence, and commitment. I call my system, 100 over 80.

100% confidence and 80% effort

Confidence and commitment.

The 100 over 80 system.

I have used this system for many years. Especially, when coaching players, for big events. It is simple, easy to remember, and therefore it works. It stands for 100% commitment, over 80% effort, equals full confidence, and a good shot. The opposite, more or less, guarantees a bad shot.

For example, imagine you are playing on a Sunday morning, it's Captains Day, 30 people are watching, and it's your turn to hit, from the first tee. You find yourself standing over the ball, with a driver in your hand, about to make your first swing of the day, and looking at trees, bunkers, water, and 20 other places, where your first shot, could ruin your day. As a result, your belief (in your decision to use the driver) is low, and your commitment is poor. The natural reaction – is to try and force a successful shot, by making the most physical effort you can, (120%, if that was possible) and get the whole thing over, as quickly as possible. Ten seconds later, and you are replacing your divot, and looking for another ball.

Alternatively, you choose a club, that you truly believe, gives you the best chance of hitting a decent shot, even if that club is only a 6-iron, or less. Now you believe you have planned an achievable shot, and you can make a calm, confident swing, using just 80% effort. The result is most likely to be, an excellent shot. The equation is simple – 100% commitment, (belief) and 80% physical effort, will result in a calm, confident swing.

I hear you ask, "I had to use a 6-iron, for my tee shot on a par four, does that mean I am a bad golfer?" My answer is no, it makes you a good golfer. You made an excellent decision, based on your skill, and it allowed you to hit a good shot. By making clever decisions, that encourage good shots, your confidence will rise throughout the round, and your play will improve. In the first example, your confidence would inevitably fall, and your golf will probably deteriorate, as the day progresses.

Let me be clear. I am not advocating, that everyone uses a 6-iron, for his, or her, first tee shot. The important thing, is the decision making process, that results in you **completely believing,** that the club, and shot, is the correct choice. That's what commitment is, and it applies to every shot you play, and every golfer, beginner to expert. For each shot you face, consider:

1. **Ability** – Can I play the shot, at least nine times out of 10?
2. **Experience** – Have I played the shot successfully, in practice?
3. **Skill** – How am I playing today – poorly, or am I on a hot streak?
4. **Circumstance** – Am I behind in a match? Do I need to shoot for a tight pin, or can I play, for the middle of the green?

Answer these questions, and the shot, and club, should choose itself. If you cannot commit to the shot, then choose another shot, change clubs, or target, until you can.

Jack Nicklaus, who won nearly 100 events, including 18 major championships, did so by making very few mental errors. However, many of those wins, were the result of the other golfers, giving away the lead in the tournament, by making mistakes.

Get committed and confident, and you could be playing better golf tomorrow.

Let the golfer inside you shine.

Because I am a professional golf coach, you may imagine, that I am always looking to change my client's swings, eliminating errors to creating perfect golfing machines. Wrong! There is much more to playing good golf, than how you swing a club. I have seen people, with superb swings, who struggle to break 100. Then I have seen other golfers, with swings that would frighten a small child, but who can break 80, every week. Admittedly, sound mechanics are important, but any changes I advise, are usually aimed at creating repeatability, and improving tempo. If you can learn to swing at a speed you can control, and get the ball, to do much the same thing each time, then you will get around the golf course, relatively unscathed. How, and what you think, along with the quality of your "short game", will then determine your scores. So, assuming that you have a reasonable golf swing, you can be pretty sure, that there is a much better golfer waiting inside you – if only you could improve your mental game. If you didn't know how bad you were, how good would you be? Let that golfer inside you shine.

Staying in the moment.

Most people can throw a ball of paper, into the waste paper basket, from 10 feet, without much thought. But what would happen, if someone promised you €10 million, if you could do it in one throw? Most people would miss. Why? Because our minds would be distracted by the end result, and forget the task at hand. Mentally, we would be spending the money, or imagining the horror of missing. A simple task becomes almost impossible, and all that has changed, is something in our mind. Great sports people are able to shut out the significance of the shot, and focus on the task at hand. This is often called "staying in the moment", but a better description would be, "staying away from the moment". For example, Brad Faxton (one of the best putters on tour – ever) says that, at the moment of striking an important putt, he doesn't care if it goes in – he just thinks about rolling the ball on line and at the correct speed. Many golfers play better, after a golf lesson, because they have something to occupy their mind for each shot. A single "swing thought", which distracts their mind, away from thinking about trees, bushes, water, and bunkers. However, after a few games, the swing changes require less thought, and the mind begins to wander – along with the ball.

Another method is to compartmentalise each shot, and each hole. For example, if you went to the driving range, and hit 100 golf shots with your 7-iron, then shot number 73, should (mentally) feel the same as shot 37, and the same should apply on the golf course. Play one shot at a time. Do not allow what happened on the last shot, affect what happens on the next shot; and do not allow what happened on the last hole affect what happens on the next hole. Finish the hole, write down your score, and forget it.

Some years ago, I was playing in a qualifying competition, at a tough course, in Suffolk, England. When I started the round, I already knew that shooting level par would be enough to get me through the local rounds, and into the finals. On the tenth hole, I was faced with a 215-yard second shot, over a lake, and into a tight pin, with absolutely no margin for error. The shot was directly into a cold wind, and required a high, soft landing, 5-wood. I had worked hard, at not knowing my score, and just playing one shot at a time, and even though I had my scorecard in my back pocket, I didn't know my score. I was aware, that I was not swinging well that day, and my back was tight, but I believed I was due to make some putts. By considering only the shot I was facing, and factoring in risk versus reward – I decided I should lay-up. So I played an 80-yard sand-wedge to the edge of the lake, followed by an 8-iron, that I hit to 16 inches, and then made an easy putt, for my par. After that, my putter warmed up a bit, and I birdied four of the next six holes, then made another, at the long par-five, seventeenth. When I checked my scorecard, after the round, I discovered that (when I was contemplating my second shot at the tenth hole), I was actually three over par. The point is, had I known my score at that time, I would have felt compelled to, "GO FOR IT", and almost inevitably, would have put the ball in the water.

Playing one shot at a time, allows you to make good tactical decisions, without being influenced, by the "heat of the moment". This does not mean being emotionally numb, indeed you should take a moment to stop, and delight in the beauty of the golf course, and enjoy every good shot you play. Just be sure to put the lid back, on your emotions, and clear your head, before you approach your next shot.

Don't be a dreamer, have a plan.

Almost every golfer wants to play better tomorrow, than they did yesterday. It's human nature to want to improve; otherwise, we would still be living in caves. In golf, sometimes improvement happens almost accidentally – for example, you try your friend's driver, and discover an additional 10 yards. But, most improvements, result from working through a good plan, and that's the part, that people find more difficult. Part of the reason is confusion, between what dreams, and goals are. The dictionary definition of a dream is, a fantasy or delusion, whereas the definition of a goal is, an aim or target. Dreams remain dreams, because we fail to create a workable plan, but goals are achievable, if they are **S.M.A.R.T.**

The acronym **S.M.A.R.T.** stands for, **S**pecific, **M**easurable, **A**chievable, **R**elevant, and **T**imescale. If your plan passes the S.M.A.R.T. test, then you are well on the way, to where you want to be.

Why have goals? Well put simply, if you don't know were you are going, how will you know when you get there? A golf course, without goals, would have no map, no tees, or greens, or flags, or numbers, it would be just a big field, with bunkers – very confusing, and not much fun! Goals are simply a map, of how you plan to get from where you are now, to where you want to end up. Goal setting is a normal, and natural way, of getting to where you want to be. But, if your plan is excessively vague, or insurmountable, then it will fail. A little effort in developing your plan will help you succeed. In training, we use the acronym S.M.A.R.T., to test the validity of any goal – here's how it works.

As an example, a recreational golfer (Brian) feels that his poor putting cost him the chance to win several competitions last year. He wants to win the Captains day prize this year. To just say, "My plan is to putt better and win Captains Day", is vague, unrealistic, and likely to fail. We cannot plan to succeed; we can only plan to do the things, which may make us successful.

Here is the S.M.A.R.T. approach:

Specific? Brian will improve his putting, by having a lesson, and practicing for 15 minutes, four evenings a week, on a putting mat.

Measurable? Brian currently averages 42 putts, in a round of golf, with four three-putts. His target is to improve to 36 putts, with no more than one three-putt, for three consecutive rounds of golf.

Achievable? This is an improvement of just six putts. With some instruction, and practice, this is a realistic target.

Relevant? Yes. A small amount of practice, will improve Brian's scoring, and improve his chance of winning competitions. By focusing on what he can do, he improves the chances of winning on Captain's Day.

Timescale? He will have a lesson, within two weeks, and then practice for four evenings a week, until he achieves his target score.

The trick is to focus on the things you can control, and not on those you can't. Then make a plan in small, measurable steps. By having a realistic plan, with measurable steps, you are much more likely to succeed. Many golfers never improve, because they simply fail to identify the easy steps required to make an improvement. If you find yourself regularly buying new clubs, or attempting drastic swing changes, then perhaps it is time to get your own "smart" plan. Objectively review your golf game, and identify one small area that could be improved. Consider if you could benefit most by improvements in putting, chipping, bunker play, iron shots, driving, your temper, your course management, fitness or flexibility. Now consider how you can improve. Do you need lessons? Can you do more practice? Should you read a book? Once you have identified what you are going to do, apply the "smart test", until you have a plan that you like. Then write it down. You don't have to show anyone, but you are much more likely to succeed, when you have committed your plan to paper. If it is a good plan, when you read back, it you will think, "Yes, that will work."

Go on, be S.M.A.R.T. and make a plan.

Consistent golf – it's a matter of routine.

Las Vegas casinos are deliberately designed, to be bright, and noisy places, which over-stimulate your mind, and disable your ability, to make good decisions. An over-stimulated mind; is a disaster waiting to happen, on the golf course, as much as it is in a casino. Most golfers can look back on bad shots, and poor decisions, and ask, "What was I thinking?" The answer is usually – not very much. The avalanche of sights, sounds, thoughts, fears and feelings, we regularly encounter while trying to play a simple golf shot, leave our minds, noisy, and unable to focus. Great golfers develop strategies to "calm" their minds, and permit clear thinking, for each shot. A sound pre-shot routine, is a large part of any good strategy. Take a little time, to develop your pre-shot routine, and your golf could become a better bet. Good luck.

Simple, but routine.

The first thing to understand is that, although we are looking at the detail here, the pre-shot routine is key, in making your golf simpler, and more consistent. It is simply a series of actions, that you complete before you play every shot. Train your mind, and learn to think, away from the course, or competitive play. On the golf course, your routine should be simple, and repetitive – something that brings comfort and calm, at times of stress. The following are the steps, or stages, that are evident in all effective, pre-shot routines.

Consistent – The familiarity of a routine, provides considerable comfort at a time of stress; any change to routine, can make the simplest action difficult. Try this experiment. Deliberately do something in your life differently – for a day. Give up the T.V. remote; try brushing your teeth (or holding your cup) with the opposite hand. Perhaps change the order with which you put your shoes on. Find something routine in your life, and change it. I guarantee, you will notice you feel a little stressed, particularly, if you choose to give up the T.V. remote! Most golfers have some sort of routine. However, when they are faced with a pressure shot, the top golfers make a conscious effort, to stick to their routine – whereas the recreational golfer, will usually, unwittingly, change their routine, by trying to "make an extra effort", with the shot. This is generally why top golfers, are better at coping with stressful situations.

Have a plan — Before you play, you should have a plan for each hole, and stick to it – although it's permissible (and a good idea), to have a contingency plan. For example, "I am going to go for the green on the par-fives with my second shot, if I am inside 220 yards. But, if I lay up, I will try and leave an 80-yard third shot". Whenever you choose the shot, or club, you are going to play – be decisive and confident, about your decision. This is much more important, than being correct. If you are in doubt, choose another club, or shot, so that you *can* feel confident about what you intend to do. It's good practice, to have a swing thought – but please, only one. Something simple like, "finish your backswing", or, "slow tempo", is fine. Complex swing mechanics are for practice only.

Picture it – Visualising the shot is important in building confidence, in your ability to play the shot. Jack Nicklaus would see the shot, exactly as if watching a film. If you can picture a successful shot clearly, several times, the effect on your confidence is the same as if you actually played it.

Practice swings – The practice swing is to reinforce the picture you have created, and to consolidate your swing thought. It is not a time to "practice" golf. Try and make your practice swings real, so you don't try and make a different swing, when the ball is present. Most pros will take exactly the same number of practice swings, for each shot.

Have a trigger – If you see a professional golfer, disturbed in the process of playing a shot, they will usually put the club back in the bag, and start again. This is because, taking the club out of the bag, is often the trigger, which "calms" their mind, before hitting the shot. Find your trigger action, or create one.

Countdown – Once over the ball, most top golfers will take exactly the same number of waggles, and looks at the target. You can usually time their countdown, to pulling the trigger, to the second, whatever the situation.

Finally – Take some time (away from competitive play), to create your own pre-shot routine, then practice it, until it is as comfortable, as how you brush your teeth.

On the course, keep it simple and routine.

You are what you think.

Whether you think you will win, or whether you think you will lose, you are probably right. In golf (and life), we usually become, what we think about ourselves. Prolific winners see themselves as winners, and they know that they will win, and they do the things that will help them to win, in the sure knowledge, that they are going to win. Look at prolific winners like, Mike Tyson, Muhammad Ali, Michael Schumacher, Jack Nicklaus and Tiger Woods. They all carry such an air of confidence, that they just look like they are going to win. You may be thinking that success can breed confidence, and it's true that it may help. But the truth is that, being a winner yesterday, does not guarantee winning today. Winners develop strategies, and tricks, that keep them in the correct frame of mind, surfing a wave of confidence, to the next win. Thinking like a winner, does not guarantee you will win, but thinking poorly, will unquestionably make you play poorly. Follow these winning strategies, and you could be the next winner.

The winning strategy.

Have a game plan – Have a plan for each hole, and every shot. Your plan should favour strategies, which are the least likely, to get you into trouble. For example, downhill putts should just fall into the front of the hole, but uphill, you can be a little more aggressive. Don't plan to hit your driver on every hole. Even the world's best with the driver have to compromise sometimes, for the sake of making a good score. Jack Nicklaus shot 63, at Firestone, using just his 3-wood, and Tiger Woods, only used his driver occasionally, to win the Open at Royal Liverpool.

Expect, and accept, mistakes – I have established course records three times, over the years, and on each occasion, I probably only hit two, or three shots, that went exactly where I intended. The remainder of the shots – were just good misses. No joke. It's not the quality of your good shots, but rather the quality of your bad shots, that defines your golf. Great golfers always have an "out", or escape plan, for every shot they hit. For example, at my club, Woodstock, if you miss most of the greens on the short side, you will have a simple uphill chip or putt. Also, learn to accept your misses. If you are a 16-handicap golfer, you can make 16 mistakes, before you have the right to get upset.

Choose your battles – Keeping your handicap, or maintaining a winning streak, is often more to do with, when you don't play, than it is about, when you do. Some courses will not fit your game. On some occasions, you may not be ready to play, competitively. Choose the time, and place, that suits you. You may be working on your swing, or feeling unwell, or just lacking the time to practice this month. Be under no illusions, great winners choose their battles.

Walk like a champion – If you see someone on the opposite fairway, with his, or her head down, and shoulders slumped, you can be pretty sure, they are having a bad day. Great winners, make an effort to look like a winner, at all times. Attitude is infectious. Try and act like you are having a great day. You will be amazed how things can turn around!

Create belief – Ordinary golfers are subconsciously waiting for the next bad shot, so they can say, "I told you so!" Winners, look for excuses to believe, that they are going to hit great shots. For example, the champion (after missing his first six putts), will think, "Statistically, the next putt must go in – I can't miss," and (after making the first six putts), "Boy, I'm hot today – I can't miss!" The club golfer, faced with the same situation, will think the exact opposite. Look for reasons to believe you are destined to hit good shots – it may seem like a trick, but it works.

Practice winning – You must visualise, winning situations. Most golfers have pretended, "This putt, to win the Open", but you need to practice situations, and challenges, that create pressure, and the feeling of winning. As a junior, I frequently played two balls, and pretended it was Nicklaus, or Palmer, or Player, against me, in matchplay. Sometimes I would even deliberately play one ball with fade, and the other, with draw. For many years, my friends and I, played each week, for the same 10 pence coin, and we played like it was a million pounds! I still have that coin.

Get to work on developing your winning strategy.

Coping with adversity.

Here is a situation that I present to many of my clients, when discussing the mental side of golf and how to cope with adversity. Imagine, for a moment, that last night God appeared to you and (for some reason) told you that today you were going to play golf and shoot a level par 71. Right now, you are out on the course. After hitting your first drive "out of bounds", topping your fifth shot into a bunker and three-putting the green, you took a horrid nine. You follow this with a six at the second to be seven over par after just two holes. Here we are on the third tee and I ask, "What are you thinking?" Almost without exception, most recreational golfers would say, "Obviously I am going to have another awful day – God must be wrong!" Of course, what you should be thinking is, "Wow – I must be about to make a sack-full of birdies and eagles over the next 16 holes. This is going to be great fun!" For some reason, golfers (in particular) are inclined to think things like, "I thought I was going to play badly and I was right!" Thinking positively does not guarantee success. You must help the situation with a sensible strategy, some common sense and (occasionally) a bit of good fortune. However, negative thinking will always achieve exactly what you expected.

Here are a few thoughts, which I have found to be helpful in over 40 years of playing golf.

Encouraging the positive.

A fear of success – I have discovered that many sports people secretly think (sometimes unconsciously) "If I expect to fail, then I won't be disappointed and embarrassed, when I play badly". This way of thinking is somehow comforting, whereas striving for success and falling short is seen as a bad thing. It is only a game, after all. Nobody died (unless you played really badly!) and it is O.K. to do your best and not win. I have had days when I shot 65 and other days, when I couldn't break 80. All I try and ask of myself is that I end the day thinking, "That was the best score I could shoot, with the game I had today". You should ask no more of yourself.

Bad shots don't make you a bad person – I find business people (especially those in sales) are inclined to judge themselves, by how well they play on the golf course. Their self-worth is directly related to the quality of their golf shots. I have been particularly guilty of this myself, thinking, "I played poorly today, I must be a bad person". We also believe others judge us on the quality of our golf. Of course most people judge us by more important things like honesty, kindness and what is in our heart, rather than our golf game. Or at least they should. Be kind to yourself – it's only a game, even if you do it for a living.

Your bad may be good – Don't get down and give up, if you are playing badly. Other golfers may, quite possibly, be having worse problems. Professional tournament golf is littered with tales of players who could have won, if only they had known that they were doing better than they thought. Don't just assume that everyone but you is delivering a faultless performance. Try and do your best – your bad day may still be better than everyone else's!

Patience is a golfer's greatest gift – Golf is a great teacher of life skills, for both adults and children. We learn honesty (because we are our own referee), good etiquette, friendship and how to count – sometimes to quite large numbers! It also teaches us that life is not always fair, or even-handed. And great golfers learn the importance of patience. For example, even the best instruction and quality practice, doesn't always yield immediate results. Like casting your fishing bait on the water, sometimes, all you can do is wait. If you have done the right things, be patient – results will come.

Anger and frustration – It can be very difficult to cope with some of the things that golf can do to us. Giving in to anger and frustration can destroy your game, because (unlike many other sports), the rush of adrenalin, will have a negative impact on your ability to think clearly, and play well. Ben Hogan used to say, "You can be suitably irritated for 10 seconds, then forget it!" I agree. Take a moment to think, "Right, that shot is over, it's gone. If I hit it last month it wouldn't be affecting me now, so really it doesn't matter". Take 10 seconds and start afresh.

Encouraging the positive.

Relish the challenge – Golf is a game of mistakes. Your golf is not measured by how good your good shots are, but by how bad your bad shots are, and how well you recover from them. Almost every shot you hit will be a little off, some more than others. So get used to it, and relish the challenge of recovering from mistakes. Be the kind of golfer who sees the ball go into the trees and thinks, "Great – now I can produce some magic, and save my par!"

Getting out of bunkers, chipping close from heavy rough, or just getting through a bad day is what this wonderful game is all about. Relish the challenge!

Lucky? – There is no such thing as "net luck". If you play golf long enough, you will get as many good bounces, as bad bounces. Although you could argue that some golfers are lucky enough to die, before they have had their share of bad bounces. Three of my close friends passed "before their time". They are missed, but not forgotten.

Everyone is watching! – When a client tells me that they worry because people may be watching, I ask, "Who are **you** watching?" Of course the answer is, nobody. We pay very little attention to others, and they return the compliment. Other people don't care how you play, as long as you are good company, and play at a reasonable pace. Enjoy the company, be polite, make sure you know where your ball went, and have fun. You don't mind if they hit a bad shot, so why should they care, if you happen to hit a shot sideways?

Relish the challenge!

Managing Your Game

It's all in the numbers!

When a new client tells me that they need to improve a certain area of their game (for example, driving), I always ask one question. How do you know? Most golfers make the mistake of linking errors to emotions, so the shot that made them most upset last week, is the thing they want to improve today. Which is fine. But fixing one swing when you shot 90, isn't going to improve your handicap very much. Before you book your next golf lesson, try recording four scorecards, and count how many shots you had in each category listed below. Then, just like this real example that follows, you will soon be able to see which area of your game needs improvement, and how many shots it may save you.

Driving

Did you drive the ball into the area you were aiming?

10/13 yes = 77%

Good for his handicap

Shots to the green

Did you hit the green when you realistically expected to?

9/18 yes = 50%

Average for handicap

Chipping & pitching

Did I hit my chips to within three feet of the hole?

1/9 yes = 11%

Very poor! Fluffed four chips and left most of them over six feet away.

Needs improvement.

Bunkers

Only one bunker shot and it was a bad lie.

0/1 = 0

Ignore

Putting

Total number of putts? 37

Needs to be less than 36.

Average number of putts taken for each birdie opportunity?

16 putts from seven chances

 = 2.3 for each G.I.R.

Should be less than 2!

Number of three putts = 2

Should be nil

Summary Mr A. Golfer	Player handicap 18	Score 89 (+18)

Analysis

Eight shots were wasted by chipping poorly.

Two shots were lost to three putts.

Four shots were lost putting for birdies.

If he just improved his putting and chipping then played the same round again, he would have scored 75!

Don't be afraid of your numbers!

I find that the score transfixes many recreational players while they are playing, but they seldom consider their statistics after the round. Whereas most professional golfers forget their score, once they have written it down, choosing instead to focus on each shot, as an "island" in the game. However, post round, the professional will carefully review each shot for quality, commitment and results, to identify where improvements can be made. We should all enjoy and remember out best shots, but I find that only the better players are readily able to consider their failings, and plan constructively for improvement. Even if you are not planning to take a course of lessons, or make additional time to practice, reviewing your statistics can improve your scores. Clearly in the real example above, some coaching and practice in chipping and putting could help (and it did!). But understanding your statistics can help in other ways. You may find that your scores would improve by putting from just off the green, rather than duffing a chip shot. Perhaps you always drop shots at par fives, by going for the big drive and would score better, if you used a 3-wood to put the ball in play. Your statistics will always help you understand your game, if you take the time to know them. After all – if you don't know what's broken, how can you fix it?

Follow the Highway Code!

All golfers make mistakes, hit bad shots and get unlucky breaks. What often separates the professional from the recreational golfer, is not following one bad shot with another. I am amazed by the number of times I have seen brilliant business people, who make excellent decisions every day, doing the most idiotic things on the golf course. I once watched a 23-handicap heart surgeon try and hit a 2 iron out of four inches of rough, across 180 yards of water, It didn't work out well! Many top golfers use the traffic light system below to help them decide how to play a shot. The trick is to play one shot at a time, not letting what happened on the last shot affect what you do with the next one. Consider each shot independently and decide if it is red, amber or green *before* you decide what to do. Try it on every shot for four rounds of golf. I guarantee you will score better.

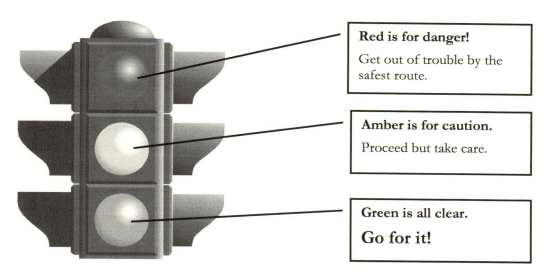

Red is for danger!

Get out of trouble by the safest route.

Amber is for caution.

Proceed but take care.

Green is all clear.

Go for it!

"We can't solve problems by using the same kind of thinking we used, when we created them". – Albert Einstein

The red light.

Your tee shot has landed deep, in thick, wet, rough. The well-bunkered green is 215 yards away, protected at the front by a pond. Many golfers, in this position, would give in to their ego and "have a rip".

The clever thing to do is:

1. Consider the penalty for not hitting the perfect shot.

2. Honestly assess how well you are playing today.

3. If you had 10 attempts, how many times would you successfully play the shot? If the answer is less than nine, then play out sideways.

Remember: never try a shot in competition that you haven't already practiced successfully several times before.

The amber light.

After your tee shot, you find the direct line to the green blocked by a group of four trees. This is a shot that requires a good decision, or good luck!

1. If the lie is poor and you are not confident you can accurately squeeze the ball low through the trees, then play out sideways.

2. If the lie is reasonable and you have practiced the shot, you may decide to play left of the trees and cut a mid iron, to advance the ball around 150 yards.

3. If your lie, swing, confidence, and ability are all good, you may decide to punch a 3-iron under the trees, and run the ball onto the green.

4. These "amber" decisions are the most important decisions of your round.

The green light.

You have just hit another excellent tee shot and your ball is sitting nicely, in the middle of the fairway.

1. You are swinging well and you are confident of which club to use.

2. The flag is accessible and a miss would leave a simple chip, or putt.

No doubts?

Go for it!

Drive carefully and arrive safe!

Many recreational golfers seem to think that every tee shot on par fours and fives, automatically requires the use of the driver. I agree that it is fun to hit the ball a long way, but only if it doesn't wreck your scorecard! Frequently, clients have asked me if not hitting your driver every time, means you are a bad golfer? My answer is that choosing when to use a driver, and when to use your 3-wood (or another club), will surely make you a better golfer. Your driver is a more difficult club to hit and therefore naturally less accurate, so correctly choosing when to use the "Big Dog" and when to leave it in the bag, is actually the sign of a good golfer. On average, most club golfers will hit more fairways with a 3-wood and as a result achieve longer drives, than a driver hit into the rough (or trees). But even if you can hit your driver pretty straight, sometimes a long drive will reach trouble, where a shorter shot will not. Next time you play, think carefully and choose the club that targets the biggest safe area for each tee shot and then, when the time is right, get out your driver and go for it. Look at the simple examples of driving strategy that follow and consider; how could you change your driving strategy? A good driver is a safe driver and a happy golfer!

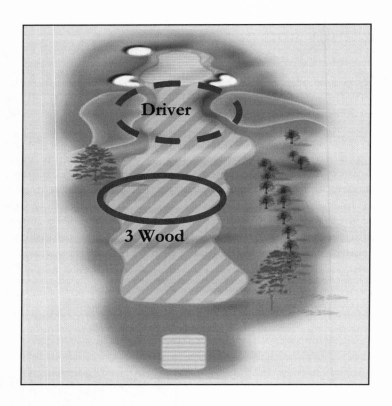

This example is of a short par four.

A well-struck driver will carry the ball to the point where the fairway is at it's most narrow, and brings the water into play. Also, even if you managed to hit the fairway, the remaining shot of 40 to 60 yards is generally too short to control effectively. Good driving strategy here is to hit a three wood. If you are thinking that getting close to the flag from 100 yards is too hard (after hitting a three wood from the tee), then you have no business trying to hit a driver at a 20-yard gap anyway!

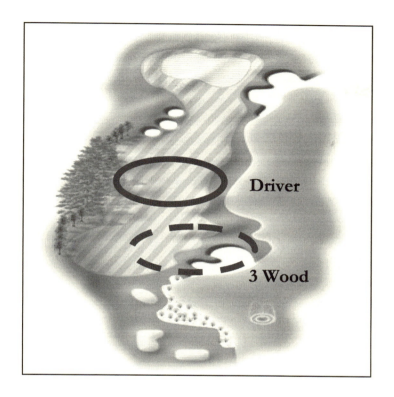

This example is a long par five.

Here the green is unreachable in two shots, so many club golfers may hit a 3-wood tee ball for "safety". Actually, in this case the driver makes more sense, as the additional length will clear the water and the bunker, where the shorter shot leaves them in play. Even if your ball landed in the water at driver length, it is likely that you will get to drop near to where it should have landed. Whereas a wet 3-wood drive may need to be re-played from the tee.

10 resolutions for better golf.

Give up smoking, get fit, lose weight, and stop believing in politicians! Do you find you start each year full of good intentions that you never keep? Most of our plans fail because we try to do too much and don't have a good plan. You can easily improve your golf by making small changes to lots of little things, rather than making a big change, to one thing. Here are "10 resolutions" you can easily commit to and quickly improve your golf for the new season.

1. Make 10 putts consecutively. In most rounds of golf, almost 50% of your shots will be putts. It is often the area of your game that can have the biggest impact on your score, with just a small improvement. For this drill, find a flat surface and putt to the hole from three feet (if you are practicing indoors on a mat or carpet, use a coin as your target). Your task is to make the putt (or hit the coin) 10 times consecutively. It's harder than you may think! This is a great drill, as by the eighth putt, the pressure is on and because you have the same putt every time, it is a test of physical skill, mechanics and mental strength. By the way, tour professionals try and make 100 consecutive putts!

2. The three-ball chip drill. This is a favourite of mine as you can do it in your garden or by the first tee, if you have 15 minutes spare. All you need is a sand-wedge and three golf balls. Chip the first ball so it finishes no more than 10 feet away. Now chip the second ball and try and land it on top of the first ball (on the first bounce), then chip the last ball and try and land it where the second ball stopped. Pick them up and do it again. This drill has the benefit of making you focus on ball flight and landing position, as well as changing the distance for every shot.

3. Leave the driver in the bag. Commit to keeping your ego under control and only using your driver, when you have hit five good tee shots with another club (the 3-wood, 5-wood or even a 5-iron if necessary). The job of the tee shot is to put the ball in a good position to play the next shot and not just to try and hit the ball further than your playing partners!

4. Play three sixes. Many golfers find themselves playing golf "cold", without the benefit of practice or a decent warm-up and not surprisingly, their day is often ruined by the fourth hole! Why not agree to play the first six holes, as practice and warm-up, and then play the remaining 12 holes seriously, as two groups of six holes. I guarantee that you will enjoy the day more and you may find that your score is better – perhaps even on the first six holes.

5. Check your fundamentals. Most golf shots go wrong before the ball is even struck. It's true! The majority of poor golf shot or swing errors have their roots in incorrect fundamentals. For example, if your aim is wrong by 30 yards and you make a perfect swing, you will miss the target by 30 yards. Then you will start trying to correct the error on your next shot by changing your swing or grip. On the next swing, you will probably add another correction and so on. This will continue until you have about 12 things you need to correct on every shot. Ironically, had your aim been corrected on the first swing, you could have had a hole-in-one! At the beginning of the year, all professional golfers see their coaches, to get their fundamentals checked, and you should do the same. Don't wait until the start of the season, call your local teaching professional (or me) and book a lesson, to get your check up on the following "non-moving parts".

Grip – Does your grip naturally return the club to the ball, with the face looking at the intended target?

Alignment – Do the lines through your feet, knees, hips, shoulders, elbows and eyes line up?

Aim – Is your body correctly aimed, parallel to your intended ball-target line?

Ball position – Is the golf ball in the correct position for the club you are intending to use, relative to your feet or chest. Get this wrong and you could slice or hook, hit the ground first or fail to get the ball into the air.

Posture – Does the body shape you create at set-up, allow you to swing correctly without "standing up"? Errors in posture can cause serious back problems, as well as damaging your golf.

6. Keep your basic statistics. "It's not what you know and it's not what you don't know. It's what you think you know, that just isn't so!" (Mark Twain) My point in using this quote is that, many golfers are unaware of where they are losing their shots and therefore, waste time practicing the wrong things. By keeping a simple record of your statistics for each round, you will be able to recognise what needs practice and track your improvement. Don't make it complicated or a chore.

At the end of each round (in the bar or when you get home), rate your shots for the following for each hole. Mark one for yes and zero for no:

Driving – Did your tee shot go to approximately the correct place? Did it lose a ball, or cost you a shot?

Shots to the green – Did you hit the green when you were (realistically) attempting to?

Scrambling – When you missed the green, or played an approach from less than 50 yards, did you get the ball within three feet?

Putting – How many putts did you have on each hole, if you had less than 36, in total? Excellent!

7. Use your handicap. Playing a medal round, what is the difference between being 16 over par and two under? Well, if you are an 18-handicap golfer it is just a matter of perspective. If you are an 18-handicap golfer trying to play the same scorecard as a scratch golfer, you will always be over par and that is mentally a very negative situation. If however, you change your scorecard (using the stroke index as you would in stableford scoring) then on a reasonable scoring day, you will be under par and feeling positive! Look at it this way. For most handicap golfers, that difficult par three now becomes a drivable par four. How much more fun is that?

8. Use a heavy club. I believe that it was "Slamming" Sam Sneed who once said "The best exercise for golf — is golf". Although I would encourage everyone to walk, run or visit the gym to improve your general health and fitness, I believe that swinging a heavy golf club (without a ball) is great for your golf. You can buy weighted clubs, but I prefer to use a spare club, like an old 3-iron, but make sure that it has a good grip. Put a small handful of sand or soil in the corner of a plastic bag and securely attach it to the clubface with strong tape to ensure it is not going to fly off! Making 20 to 30 slow, full, practice swings each day (in both directions), will improve your strength and flexibility. Make an additional 10 swings where you go at full speed through the pretend hitting area, and you will quickly find you gain a few yards on your drives.

9. Use the 10-second rule. Most recreational golfers permit one bad shot to affect their mood (and scoring) for the remainder of the round, and professionals are not immune to this malaise! I encourage my clients to apply the "10 second rule". I tell him or her to remember that it is only a game and (hopefully) nobody died. Then, you are permitted to be "suitably irritated" for only 10-seconds or, if you prefer, the next 10 steps. After that, hit the delete button and start the next shot with a calm cool head.

10. Get a lesson. Far too many golfers wait until they start playing in the new season, before they book some lessons – then they are trying to compete and make swing changes, at the same time. That is hard work for them – and me! I recommend that you get your "golf tune up" before the race begins. Secondly, when you have a lesson you must commit to actually making changes, and making the time and effort to practice, until the changes stick. Otherwise, you are not giving yourself, or your professional, the opportunity and space to achieve value for money. If you really want a quick improvement with minimum effort, book a shortgame lesson and sharpen up your scoring.

Go on – give it a try!

Get fit for golf.

Preparation is only obvious by its absence! You may see a thousand cars on your drive to work tomorrow, but you will only notice the guy who forgot to check he had enough fuel for his trip. There are many things that you can do to that will help you play better golf, that do not involve swing rebuilds, or hours of practice. I frequently see club golfers (and the occasional professional) waste shots by not having the correct equipment, failing to prepare correctly, not knowing the rules and many other simple mistakes. Here are a few basic things that you should be doing, if you are going to have the best opportunity, to play good golf.

Good preparation

Fluids – Thirst is a very poor indicator of hydration; most people will loose two to three per cent of their body's fluid level, before they start to feel thirsty. This can cause a drop in electrolytes, which can result in bad coordination and mental mistakes. Drink fluids before, during and after your game, even if you don't feel any need. There are many types and makes of "sport drinks" that offer magical hydration properties. After many years of research, I have discovered that the best product is called "WATER"!

Food – "A hungry dog hunts better, but a full stomach leaves no room for butterflies". I recommend that you have a good breakfast, before you play and lunch, if you are playing late. Feel free to eat as much as you like while you are playing golf, as it is very important to keep your energy up. Your diet can take a break while you are having a little exercise, but avoid sugary bars. Take the time to make some healthy sandwiches and take some bananas, as they are good for providing long lasting energy.

Equipment – I have no doubt that improvements in golf equipment and the application of technology has helped the professional game. In particular, changes to the ball and driver have helped the top players hit the ball exceptional distances. However, as average handicaps are unchanged for 20 years, the effect on the amateur game is almost zero; although anyone who bought a €500 driver will always tell you it has revolutionised their game! What has really helped both recreational and professional golfers play better, are improvements in the technical knowledge and teaching skills of golf coaches, combined with the use of high-speed video cameras and computer analysis – but you would expect me to say that! The fact is that most club golfers would play just as well, if they had budget clubs without the big brand name, as long as they were in decent condition. Clean your clubs once a week and give the grips a wash each month, with hand soap and warm water, it will keep them "tacky" and extend their life. If your grips are slick, hard or cracked get them replaced by a competent professional, the cost is minimal – I only charge from €5 a club. If you want to spend a little money, buy some quality rainwear and if, like me, your hands slip on the club when wet, get some all weather gloves for both hands. It's a good idea to have a hand towel and a few spare gloves in a plastic bag, in the pocket of your golf bag. Your wet weather game will improve and you may be more inclined to play all year around. Other things to carry are: extra tees, ball markers, a rulebook, plasters, sun block and a pitch mark repairer. I don't care which brand of golf ball you play as long as you can afford to loose a few, and all the balls you use are the same model. Many players subconsciously get tense over a tight tee shot, because of the cost of the ball. Most manufacturers produce a range of balls to suit most pockets and I can assure you, better players can play just as well with a mid-price ball. It can take a couple of weeks to get completely used to a different golf ball and that is why, I hate to see any player, with a bag full of various "lake balls", which they swap around on every hole. The feel, spin and hardness of different golf ball brands, can differ considerably, sometimes by as much as 10 yards, for identical shots. No golfer can cope with that, so find a ball you like, and can afford, then stick to it!

Good preparation.

Pre-game practice? – I see a high percentage of recreational players who arrive at the first tee at a run, directly from their cars, frequently still conducting business on the mobile phone. Their hearts are probably pounding, with their stress levels through the roof. And that is before they hit the first shot out of bounds! If you are going to make time to play golf then MAKE TIME! At worst, you should arrive 45 minutes early, switch off your mobile phone, get all your kit out and ready, pay your fees, book in and so on. That should leave you 25 minutes to have a stretch with some practice swings, and then hit a few chips and putts. I like to lay a shaft along my target line and putt from three to four feet, so I can make sure my aim and club path are

correct. A good idea is to putt from close enough to make all the putts. That way you build confidence. Also, try putting to a coin before you play, then out on the course the hole will look like a bucket – it's great!

Develop a little pre-game routine of cleaning and checking equipment the night before. Then hitting chips and putts, just before you tee off. Whatever you do, do not change your routine for a big event, it only adds to the pressure and stress.

Golf shoes – Good golf shoes are important because on most courses you will walk approximately five miles during a round. Make sure that your shoes are in decent condition, clean, with all the studs in place and not excessively worn. Buying a high quality shoe can be a good investment, as they will last if you look after them well. However, if you play golf little and often, there is some logic in buying a lower cost shoe, and replacing them more frequently.

Golf clubs – The rules of golf state that you can only carry 14 clubs in your golf bag, but that doesn't mean you have to! I have around 20 clubs that I can choose from, depending on which course I am playing and the conditions. My normal set will be driver, a strong 5-wood, a 7-wood that carries as far as a 2-iron but lands softer, a 4-hybrid, numbers 5 to 9 irons, four wedges and a putter. In wet conditions I will swap my lob wedge for a 3-wood because, with the greens being wet and soft, I can stop the ball fine with a sand-wedge, but I may need the additional length of the 3-wood for some shots. On some courses or on windy days, I may replace the 7-wood and hybrid with my regular 3 and 4-irons.

Some professionals like to keep a heavy putter for putting on fast greens and a light putter for slow greens; others prefer to do the opposite. Whatever you do, it is good to have the option to swap clubs. Keep a few spare clubs in the boot of your car, and then if you arrive to play and the wind has got up, you can choose a different weapon for the battle to come.

One other piece of advice – never discard an old putter. If you loose your touch it can help to go back to a once loved friend, it's amazing how quickly your feel will return.

Get ready for golf.

Buying clubs – Eventually, every golfer will buy new equipment. Golf is the worst sport for "boys' toys" and in the good years, many players are encouraged to buy new equipment (almost every week) in the search for better, longer, straighter or higher shots. Here are some things to weigh up:

Custom fitting – Never buy before you consider getting custom fitted clubs; ill-fitting or inappropriate clubs have ruined many golf games. Having correctly fitted clubs can ensure your new clubs work for you and not against you. The picture below is computer analysis data from a driver fitting; this level of data can help you get a driver that will maximise your distance and accuracy. Most recreational golfers play with drivers that are more appropriate for top professionals, but their ego lets them think that playing with a stiff shafted 9-degree driver will improve their scores, when they hold an 18-handicap and cannot consistently hit a green with a 7-iron.

	Launch						Flight	Landing Flat				
Club	Club Speed	Ball Speed	Smash Factor	Vert. Angle	Horz Angle	Spin Rate	Max Height	Carry Flat	Side Flat	Vert. Angle	Ball Speed	Flight Time
	[mph]	[mph]	[]	[deg]	[deg]	[rpm]	[m]	[m]	[m]	[deg]	[mph]	[s]
1w	113.2	169.0	1.49	10.9	3.6 L	2418	31.0	235.8	4.9 L	45.3	61.5	6.96
1w	111.6	170.9	1.53	11.7	0.8 R	2429	33.2	254.8	12.0 R	43.7	64.3	7.25
1w	111.4	168.7	1.51	12.8	2.0 L	1860	30.5	245.0	2.0 L	41.7	63.9	6.76
1w	111.6	168.4	1.51	11.9	1.3 L	2461	30.4	245.2	10.1 L	41.6	65.7	6.74

Changing clubs – It can take a professional several months to get fully comfortable with a new set of irons, yet some amateur players seem to change clubs every three months. Get professional advice before you change your clubs, or better yet, get some lessons first.

Putters – Your putter is your most important club. Many club players would never consider paying €100 for a putter, but they think that the latest driver is a "must have", regardless of cost. Yet they use their putter, for up to four-times as many shots as their driver. The right putter is worth paying a bit extra for. Every golfer, regardless of ability, should have a putter that fits their body and stroke, rather than trying to fit their body and stroke to a putter built for a taller person. Fitting a putter is quick and usually cost around €20 to €50, but the improvement could save you eight to 10 shots a round.

Know the rules – Unlike any other sport I am aware of, in golf the player is responsible for making decisions about rules and calling penalties, when required. The *Rules of Golf* is published by the R&A and available free of charge at most good golf shops. Get one and keep it in your bag. It is easy to use and most situations can be resolved by looking in the index and following the sub-headings. There are a few things to keep in mind. First, a good understanding of the rules can save you a lot of shots over time, without taking any unfair advantage. Second, check the back of the scorecard for "local rules", like which paths and ditches are in play; also check notice boards for temporary rules – like "clean and place". Third,

many big money sports have suffered almost laughable rules infringements that were missed by the referee, whereas golf has a proud tradition of fair play – which every player (including you) must try and uphold.

Lastly, it is embarrassing and frustrating for you and your playing partners, if someone has to point out an infringement of the rules which, with a little effort you could and should have been aware of. As a junior, I played in a father and son matchplay event, where I witnessed one of our eight-handicap opponents demonstrate a disastrous breach of the rules. He was last to play and facing a tricky downhill putt, to extend the match. To everyone's horror, he putted his ball from the fringe to his ball marker (taking four putts), before placing his ball and preparing for his putt. Fortunately his playing partner, the son, had a better understanding of the rules, and called the penalty to concede the match and avoid further embarrassment, as his father was also club captain!

Know your distances – Most club players would save shots on every round by knowing two things: how far they are from where they want to hit the ball and what club will get them there consistently. I know from conducting thousands of "playing lessons", where I take a client out on the course for a few holes, that most players take little notice of how far away from the target they are, and have no real idea of what club to hit. If you take the time to work out the distance of each shot, you will quickly find out how far you can really hit each club. Most golf courses these days have yardage charts available, or at least provide distance markers, to indicate how far it is to the centre or front of the green.

Progressive golf clubs now permit the use of GPS and laser range finders, even in competition. This is within the rules of golf (provided it is approved by the competition committee) and is a good thing because, these technologies provide information that is legally available from other sources, and it saves time. So, if you can afford a GPS, and they cost as little as €99, then get one. By the way, just because you saw a tour professional on television hit a 7-iron 205 yards; it doesn't mean you can try to do the same thing.

The weather, seasons and ground conditions can have a huge influence on the ball. I know one par-3 in England that is 215 yards, and on one winter's day, playing directly into the teeth of the wind, I was unable to reach with a well-struck driver. But six months later I made a hole-in-one, hitting downwind – with a pitching wedge!

I don't care which club you hit, as long as it goes the correct distance!

Be ready for golf.

Have a plan and stick to it! – With a little thought you should be able to come up with a realistic plan for each hole you are going to play, particularly if you play the same course most of the time. Here are several simple things you can consider in your plan, to improve your chances of scoring better.

Par fives – You do not need to hit driver on every par five. If you have no prospect of reaching the green in two shots, then hitting a 3-wood may put you in the fairway more often and result in a better score. Decide how close to a par five green you will need to be, before you will commit to "go for it" and if you are going to lay up, what is the optimum distance for you to hit your wedge?

Par fours – Which holes provide the best opportunity for making birdies and which have the biggest threat of making bogey, or worse? Some holes will provide the best score on average if you are aggressive, while others are just a matter of survival and hoping you get a lucky putt for a par.

Par threes – Some short holes offer a realistic chance to make par, while others are really just a drivable par four for most recreational players. Even for the professionals, most par threes average over par.

Driving strategy – You should begin each round with a plan that includes which club you intend to hit for each drive. I encourage my clients to plan a "bailout" for every shot, to a place where you can realistically still make a score. For example, missing the drive 50 yards right could leave you on the next fairway, with a clear shot to the green, but missing left will risk going out of bounds. Being aware of your **safety zone** will subconsciously help your misses to go that way. Tiger Woods frequently seems to get "lucky" with wild drives, but he is just very good at planning the best place to miss, if things go wrong.

Approach shots – Take time to get familiar with the greens at your course and decide where you would prefer to putt from, if you had the choice. Generally you would like to have a straight up hill putt, so consider how you can achieve that more frequently. Also, if you miss the green, where is the easiest place to chip from? Finally, making sure you take an extra club when playing over water can save you shots, that you would usually squander.

Stick to it – Sticking to a plan does not mean being inflexible; a good plan should always include alternatives and options. For example, you could decide to hit your drive with a 5-wood at a particular par four, but plan to change to driver if the hole is down wind and you feel you are swinging well. Not changing a plan means not throwing it away just because you had three bad holes. The good plan you had for the next hole is still a good plan, so stick to it!

Keep fit and healthy – The best exercise for golf is golf. Don't smoke or drink to excess if you want to play well; eat well and your body will thank you. Use a good sunscreen every time you play and wear a hat; these days there is no excuse for failing to take precautions against sun damage. I am over 50 but still hit the ball a good distance and play without pain. I am very flexible and quite strong but I don't visit the gym every day, although that should not stop you if you enjoy working out. I stretch regularly and use a heavy club to help my strength and flexibility; making sure I swing both right and left handed to balance my stretching. Other than that, I walk (fast) every day before I go to the golf course and I always walk on the golf course – I hate riding on a buggy. Core muscle strength is important to protect and support your back, so I also do regular sit-ups and press-ups. Golf is good exercise for most people, but I believe that you can improve your game and the prospect of playing into old age by keeping as fit as you can.

Know your swing – Most top players know surprisingly little about the golf swing, but are usually pretty knowledgeable about their own swings, in particular the things that go wrong. One benefit of taking golf lessons from a competent golf teaching professional is that, although you may not completely cure your swing faults, you could develop an understanding of what goes wrong, why and how to fix it during a game. Most golfers have a tendency to hook, or slice, under pressure and they usually build some compensation into their game. For example, Arnold Palmer's swing was very much "anti-left". He also knew that he tended to block the ball to the right when trying to hit a long drive, consequently, and because he knew his game, when going for the big drive, Arnold aimed down the left side and blocked the ball into the fairway. Your golf is not measured by the quality of your good shots, but by the damage caused by your bad shots. Getting to know your game could help to eliminate your errors and improve your scores.

The Next Generation

Junior Golfers

Take the easy path to a good golfing future.

Junior golfers (and adult beginners) have just one chance to get their golf game on the correct path, before swing faults become engrained and difficult to shift. I have been coaching junior golfers for over 30 years and, above all, one thing is clear; it is a fun and painless process encouraging young golfers to do the right things in golf. With correct coaching and encouragement, learning to play is just a big game. Making changes, later in life, becomes much more difficult for both teacher and student, particularly if someone has learned to play (poorly) with a swing that looks like they are trying to kill a snake in a telephone box! Golf is also a wonderful sport to help any young person develop their personality and good social qualities.

As an individual game, played in groups, it provides the opportunity to interact, play and compete in a group, but still shine as an individual. Golf teaches good manners, honesty, confidence, a sense of achievement, as well as lessons in humility and being magnanimous in victory. Oh – and it's great fun as well.

The days when golf was the preserve of the rich and privileged have passed. For example, I run a junior academy every Saturday for just €15, green-fees for a round of golf are from €20, junior memberships are available for under €250 and a decent set of starter clubs can usually be borrowed or purchased locally for less than the cost of a computer game. We have a great history of golfing achievement in Ireland. With three Major championship wins, our most successful sportsman ever; is a golf professional – Padraig Harrington.

Junior golf should be encouraged. Let's get the next generation of golfers started on the right path!

Junior golf basics.

I never forget that golf is a game, so I endeavour to make coaching fun for my juniors, by playing little games and including coaching challenges. I strongly believe that a little competition is a good thing, and that it is ok to learn at an early age that we don't always win, even if we did all the right things. Here are a few "essentials" for beginner golfers.

Good foundations – If you have a decent grip on the club, can aim it in the right direction, and are able to stand to the ball in a fashion that you can maintain throughout your swing – then you have a decent chance of hitting a good shot.

Swing, don't hit! – We call a golf swing a "swing" because that is what it does, otherwise it would be called a hit. I encourage my juniors to swing the club and just let the ball get in the way.

Start at the end – If you begin by learning to putt and chip well, then you are gifted with the ability to score. That creates the space in your game and therefore the time, to develop a good swing.

Learn to compete – A little bit of competition is a good thing, particularly if it is part of a game. It doesn't matter if you compete against a friend for a euro while you practice, or play two balls (one against the other) on your own. Any competition will sharpen you game and your mind.

Head games – If you think you are going to hit a bad shot, you probably will. Even when I teach children as young as six, I will still talk about mind management (in a simple way) because, I believe that thinking the correct way, even at an early age, can make golf more enjoyable and help you play better. Children are very good at learning skills like visualisation and pretending that a bad shot didn't happen, and an early start builds confidence that will last a lifetime.

Get involved – Join in junior competitions and coaching events. Getting involved at an early stage is excellent experience of playing in groups, competing and having fun.

Acknowledgements

No author can successfully write a book, without the support and encouragement of a lot of people, so I would like to acknowledge those people who should take some of the credit for the support I have received in writing this book. The list of helpful friends is long and they know who they are, but here are just some of them.

First, I would like to thank Joe Ó'Muircheartaigh and Noel Barrett from the "Clare People" newspaper, for their help and support and for publishing my "To the Fore" instructional series over the last 2 years.

I am forever grateful to Christy, Sheila and Avril Guerin of Woodstock golf and country club, Ennis, for providing a new home for my golf teaching services when I moved to Ireland, and allowing the use of the course, in the making of this book. In addition, I would like to thank the committee for supporting my Junior Coaching programme. I would also like to thank the thousands of golfers, who have carefully followed my teaching over the years and, through their efforts and success, proved it to be sound.

The task of completing a book of this type has been made far easier by Gabrielle Warnock and Richard Clarke proof reading, editing, and giving guidance on structure and content. Thank you both.

I also want to thank the many golf teachers and professionals that I have watched and talked with over the years about swing technique, drills and teaching methods, along with those who have encouraged and influenced me. Here are a few of their names: Bill Abbott, Shane Diles, Tony Parcell, Jon Bevan, Richard Clarke, Dr Paul Hurrion, Gerry O'Gorman and Martin Toner. Some of the great players and teachers who have inspired me over the years are Jack Nicklaus, Lee Trevino, Gary Player, Sam Snead, Nick Faldo, Jim McLean, Jimmy Ballard, Bob Toski, Jack Grout, Jim Flick, Harvey Penick, Butch Harmon, Dave Pelz, John Jacobs and many others. All better men than me, I am sure!

Finally, I want to give a special thank you to my wife and daughter, for being there.

2759752R00120

Printed in Great Britain
by Amazon.co.uk, Ltd.,
Marston Gate.